THE

BETTER WITNESS HANDBOOK

A Guide for Testifying at a Deposition, Hearing, or Trial

Angela M. Dodge, Ph.D. and John H. Ryan, Ph.D.

Litigation Psychologists

DODGE CONSULTING & PUBLICATIONS, LLP

Dodge Consulting & Publications, LLP
14591 Wiley Lane SE
Olalla, WA 98359
(253) 857-7716
www.dodgeconsulting.com
adodge@dodgeconsulting.com or jryan@dodgeconsulting.com

For more information about publications available through Dodge Consulting & Publications LLP, please visit the website at www.dodgepublications.com.

Copyright © 2013 by Dodge Consulting & Publications, LLP
Cover and text design by Kathy Campbell
Edited by Barbara Fandrich

Printed by Gorham Printing, Washington State
Printed in the United States of America
First Printing: July 2013

Print Edition ISBN 978-0-9777511-9-8
EPUB Edition ISBN 978-0-9777511-2-9
Kindle Edition ISBN 978-0-9777511-7-4

DEDICATION

This handbook is dedicated to the late Margaret Fahn.
She was a strong believer in being prepared for whatever
challenging endeavor you were about to face, whether you
were looking forward to it or you were fearful or anxious
about it. And she was an expert at preparing one of the
authors to write this handbook.

Other books available from
Dodge Consulting & Publications LLP

Preparing Witnesses to Give Effective Testimony: The Attorney's Essential Guide by Angela M. Dodge, Ph.D. and John H. Ryan, Ph.D. (April, 2013). Available through www.dodgepublications.com or by contacting adodge@dodgeconsulting.com. Also available through www.amazon.com in paperback or e-book form.

ISBN 978-0-9777511-6-7 ($24.95 plus S&H)

When Good Doctors Get Sued: A Practical Guide for Physicians Involved in Malpractice Lawsuits by Angela M. Dodge, Ph.D. in collaboration with Steven F. Fitzer, J.D. (Fourth Printing, 2012). Available through www.dodgepublications.com or by contacting adodge@dodgeconsulting.com. Also available through www.amazon.com.

ISBN 978-0-9777511-0-5 ($24.95 plus S&H)

Opening Statements-Closing Arguments by Ronald J. Matlon, Ph.D. (Second Edition, 2009). Available through www.dodgepublications.com or by contacting adodge@dodgeconsulting.com. Also available through www.amazon.com.

ISBN: 978-0-9777511-3-6 ($19.95 plus S&H)

Winning at Jury Selection: A Handbook of Practical Jury-Focused Techniques & Strategies by Angela M. Dodge, Ph.D. (July, 2010). Available through www.dodgepublications.com or by contacting adodge@dodgeconsulting.com. Also available through www.amazon.com.

ISBN 978-0-9777511-4-3 ($34.95 plus S&H)

CONTENTS

ACKNOWLEDGMENTS

Much of what we know about preparing witnesses to give testimony we have learned from the thousands of witnesses and hundreds of attorneys with whom we have worked for nearly two decades. Some witnesses have posed great challenges; others have taught us a thing or two. Some witnesses have been open and receptive to learning how to communicate more effectively; others have been impeded in the learning process by their fears about the litigation process itself. Some have made great improvements in their communication effectiveness; others have been hindered in their efforts by anxiety and personality factors outside of anyone's control. We wish to thank all of them for providing such a breadth of opportunity to us as consultants.

A large debt of gratitude is owed to Carl Mendenhall (Worden Thane law firm, Missoula, MT) and Bertha Fitzer (Fitzer Law, Tacoma, WA), two outstanding attorneys who carefully and graciously reviewed an early draft of this handbook. Both of them have impressive experience preparing witnesses, and both are competent writers in their own right. They kept us from some potentially embarrassing errors, and they clarified legal procedures we did not understand completely. This handbook is better as a result of their efforts. Thank you, Carl and Bertha.

We are also indebted to our friend and editor extraordinaire, Barbara Fandrich. We have benefited greatly from her attention to detail and uncanny wisdom about how to best communicate our experience and ideas to readers. Her sensitive and insightful contributions have made this book so much better than it might have been. Our sincere gratitude, Barbara.

CAVEATS

Many Differences Exist

There are considerable differences in how depositions, trials, and hearings are conducted throughout the country. There are geographic differences, procedural differences, and many variations in style and process. In this book we focus on some of the more common strategies and techniques, and they may not fit your particular state or area. Your attorney should be considered the final authority.

Follow Your Attorney's Advice First

This handbook is intended to supplement and complement the advice witnesses will be given by their own attorneys. The information we offer is not intended to replace the advice of one's own counsel. If there is a contradiction between the information offered in this handbook and the advice and guidance provided by your own attorney, get clarification from your attorney and follow his or her advice first. Not all of our suggestions are appropriate in all cases or all situations; your attorney knows the specifics of your case best.

Examples Are Not Intended to Coach or Script

Throughout this handbook, we provide many question-and-answer scenarios to give you concrete illustrations of rules, procedures, styles, and strategies that apply in depositions or at trial. It is not our intent in these examples to coach or script answers for witnesses, nor do we suggest you memorize the answers we have used in various examples. Our foremost rule is that every answer you give in a deposition or at a hearing or trial must be your own.

INTRODUCTION

WHO SHOULD READ
THIS BOOK, AND WHY

In the past few decades we have seen an explosion of legal challenges, including class action lawsuits, government investigations, product liability lawsuits, and personal injury litigation. With this upsurge has come a great increase in the number and variety of people who are called on to give testimony as witnesses in legal actions. As a result, a large number of people who have never before been witnesses, including ex-president Bill Clinton, television personalities, and various religious figures, have had to take the oath to tell the truth, the whole truth, and nothing but the truth. Few of them were adequately prepared to do so.

Worries of the Unprepared Witness

If you received this handbook from your attorney, you are likely preparing to testify at a hearing, to have your deposition taken, or to give testimony as a witness in a trial, and you are seeking guidance on how to navigate this unknown territory. You may be worried that you won't be sufficiently prepared for court, or that you will unknowingly say or do something to hurt your case. Even people who have experience with the judicial system can experience sleepless nights worrying about the challenge of having to give a deposition in an adversarial process, appear in court to argue one's claims or defend oneself, or testify convincingly in a legal setting of some type. You may have wondered if there is any help for the legally naïve and if so, where to find it. You have picked up the right book—help is here.

You May Be the Exception

Not all witnesses-to-be are nervous and anxious. You may be looking forward to the opportunity for your day in court. Rather than feeling anxious, you may be excited in anticipation of finally getting to tell your story of what happened. You may feel ready and able to take the witness seat and lay out your side of the disagreement.

Your excitement and confidence will undoubtedly be encouraging to the attorney, and it will make your preparation easier than if you are anxious and reluctant. However, there are some cautions. High levels of emotion, whether positive or negative, can be a hindrance. Overly enthusiastic witnesses can be poor listeners, and in your haste to tell all, you may fail to listen carefully to questions. You may become so focused on framing your answers to your best advantage that you fail to respond to what is actually being asked. You may become frustrated if the content and progress of opposing counsel's questions do not follow the pattern you expected. At trial, you could over-anticipate your own attorney's questions and break up his or her well-planned questioning sequence. Even if you are feeling ready to face your adversaries, it would be wise to read and follow the suggestions in this book in order to avoid inevitable pitfalls.

What You Can Expect from This Book

This publication is packed with information every witness should know about basic steps in the litigation process and what to expect at various stages. It includes suggestions about how to listen effectively and recognize various kinds of questions, tips on how to make a good first impression, and ideas about how to manage the anxiety and emotion that often accompanies involvement in a legal conflict. It provides many question-and-answer examples to teach you how to give effective answers to difficult questions and how to prevent anyone from putting words in your mouth or twisting your testimony unfairly. It will help you become a more confident, credible, and effective witness.

Companion Book for Your Attorney

Your attorney knows that an important key to winning any case is to make certain that every witness put on the stand is well prepared to give effective, truthful testimony. While good attorneys know the importance of adequately preparing a witness for a deposition, hearing, or trial, they may disagree about how to accomplish that goal. For this reason, we have written a companion book specifically for attorneys (*Preparing Witnesses to Give Effective Testimony: The Attorney's Essential Guide.* ISBN 978-0-9777511-6-7). Maximum benefit is achieved when you and your attorney use the guidebooks and work together to assure you are receiving the best preparation possible.

This book is not a *replacement* for good preparation by your attorney. It is designed to help those who may not have access to such preparation, and for those circumstances in which an attorney is unable to provide the concentrated preparation that is needed. It may also be a good refresher for those more experienced in giving testimony in a legal case, and for expert witnesses preparing for trial.

Selecting Appropriate Chapters

Much of the guidance we provide in this book is applicable whether you are preparing to give a deposition or testify at a hearing, arbitration, or trial. However, certain rules that apply at a deposition are different from the ground rules of giving testimony at trial. The point is that deposition testimony and trial testimony are different. If you are preparing for a deposition, you may want to skip Chapter 5 (Testifying at Trial). If you are preparing for trial, you may wish to skip Chapter 3 (About Depositions) and Chapter 4 (Giving a Deposition), as these deal primarily with questioning at a deposition. With the exception of Chapter 13 (Testifying as an Expert), all of the other chapters apply, whether you are preparing for a deposition or trial.

CHAPTER 1

SO YOU'RE GOING
TO BE A WITNESS

No one wakes up one morning with a burning desire to be a witness in any kind of legal process. It will involve lawyers (who you are not certain you can trust completely), legal language (which is Greek to anyone who has not been to law school), legal rules (which can be confusing even to attorneys), and the need to speak convincingly in front of total strangers (which gives most people a case of nervous stomach). All in all, it's a fairly stressful situation.

Even the language is intimidating—testifying, cross-examination, deposition—these all sound as if you are being interrogated. While attorneys use this language every day, it is foreign to you. And what is more frightening and intimidating than the unknown?

The Importance of a Reality Check

Despite what you may have learned about the law from television programs, as a witness you will be in an unfamiliar environment, participating in an unfamiliar process, with unfamiliar language and procedures. The entire communication situation is unusual: it is not a conversation, but a difficult question-and-answer format that feels more like an oral examination than a fact-finding process. Add to that the frightening suspicion that a clever attorney will trick you into saying something you don't mean, plus our often unrealistically high self-expectations that we should know all the right answers and perform perfectly. And let's not forget our fear of failed memories, or worse yet, our fear of hurting the case. Who wouldn't be anxious?

Although you may be scared out of your wits initially, let's get practical and realistic. Chances are that with some preparation, you will do just fine. Your memory will be better than you imagined, the questioning attorney won't be nearly as intimidating as you feared, and you will most likely listen and respond more carefully than you thought you would. It is very likely that in retrospect you could have given better, more complete answers to some questions, but most questions were answered sufficiently well. It is very unlikely you have torpedoed the case because you gave a few imperfect answers. Appreciate the difficulty of what you are being asked to do, allow yourself some level of anxiety, and do your best. Remember that the attorney who is questioning you is probably nervous too!

The Importance of Telling the Truth

Before any testimony is given, a witness is first sworn to tell the truth. This may appear to be just another legal formality, but it should be taken seriously and literally. The law is not tolerant of those who stretch, shave, exaggerate, omit, or downplay the truth. There are criminal penalties for committing perjury, which means making false statements under oath. And just as your mother may have warned: telling the truth always makes it easier to remember. When you tell the truth, you need not worry about inconsistencies or conflicting versions that may be pointed out later. There is simply nothing more convincing than the truth, the whole truth, and nothing but the truth.

Telling the truth effectively also means you must talk about only what you distinctly remember seeing, hearing, or doing. You should not embellish the facts, fill in memory gaps, guess, speculate, or talk too much. A shrewd attorney may try to bully or goad you into saying more than you should—to get you to exaggerate, add to your answer, include a little white lie, or make up something. You may comply in order to get him or her to move on. Resist this temptation. If the attorney becomes frustrated, remember that it is your credibility on the line, not his or hers.

After delivering verdicts, jurors are often asked their reactions to various witnesses, and they nearly always comment about the perceived truthfulness or honesty of the person giving the testimony they heard at trial. To judge the truthfulness of a witness's testimony, they rely not only on what is said, but how the witness delivers the answer: Did he look us in the eye when giving the answer? Did she stammer or fidget when asked a difficult question? Did his body language seem defensive? Did her eyes dart around the room? Did he always look to his attorney for cues about how to answer?

Being a well-prepared witness means more than reviewing the facts as you recall them. It must also include a focus on the non-verbal cues that signal the truthfulness of your answers. You will learn in this book how to tell the truth most effectively.

The Importance of a Good First Impression

All judges and jurors, because of their backgrounds and life experiences, are predisposed to trust some witnesses and not others. In a courtroom, jurors must rely on rather quick judgments and verbal and behavioral cues to determine who is trustworthy, who is believable. Therefore, it is critical to create a good first impression with jurors. This builds the initial trust and credibility required for jurors to believe your testimony, your evidence, and your case over that of the opposition. If you are unable to create a positive first impression with jurors, all the sound evidence and all the brilliant arguments your attorney makes will be defeated.

As it turns out, how others perceive us has less to do with content than with delivery. In fact, the majority of communication occurs at the non-verbal level. This means that body language, facial expressions, tone of voice, eye contact, rate of speech, posture, and a host of other non-verbal signals are important factors in whether others will believe you and find your testimony persuasive. Your attorney knows that your preparation must include a focus not only on *what* you say, but *how* you say it. You will learn in this book how to make a good first impression.

How Judges and Jurors Process Your Testimony

Juries and judges process the information you are giving them through two pathways—first at the intuitive or instinctive level, and then at the cognitive or mental level. Jurors have often told us that they simply "got a feeling" about a witness that made them either attentive to the witness's testimony, or caused them to tune out or discount it. If the testimony did not resonate at the instinctive level, it rarely became logged in at the reasoning or mental level. It is at the instinctive level that jurors weigh factors such as likeability, credibility, and honesty. Only after testimony passes the credibility sniff test is it processed mentally and stored for use in deliberations. In this book you will learn how to project credibility and likeability so your testimony will get heard.

Once jurors and judges have heard what you have to say, they must also understand it, believe it, and recall it. In order to be understood, it is important for witnesses to speak in common terms and avoid professional jargon and acronyms known only to you and your colleagues. For jurors and judges to believe testimony, the witness must be concerned with how the testimony is delivered. Lastly, in order for jurors and judges to recall what you have said, it must be made memorable. In this book you will learn how to ensure your testimony is effective by making certain it is not only heard, but understood, believed, and recalled during deliberations.

How Attorneys and Jurors Read Your Behavior

People are not always aware of how their behavior is being interpreted or read by someone else. Attorneys and jurors are usually quite good at reading non-verbal cues and behaviors, and they often make judgments about a witness's credibility and juror appeal on the basis of demeanor and body language. The following table suggests ways in which your behavior and communication patterns might make a negative impression on attorneys, jurors, and judges.

If Your Behavior or Demeanor Is...	Others Could Conclude You Are...
Abrupt or long-winded answers	Defensive; have something to hide
Rigid posture; sarcastic; loud voice	Angry; condescending
Lack of eye contact; many "um" and "ah" vocal fillers	Insecure; guilty; no confidence
Willing to guess or speculate	Sloppy; poor attention to detail; inattentive
Repeated requests for clarification; submissive; indirect	Incompetent
Agreeable; overly-friendly; overly-pleasing	Easy to manipulate
Dependent on documents; frequent use of "I don't know" or "I don't recall"	Poor memory; not prepared
Speaking at a very fast pace	Careless; impatient; attempting to talk your way out of it
Rush to answer; interrupts questioner	Impatient; rude

Judges and jurors will also make positive attributions concerning your demeanor. The following table suggests ways in which your behavior and communication patterns are likely to make a positive impression on attorneys, jurors, and judges.

When You...	Others Will Assume You Are...
Take pauses before speaking	Precise; thoughtful; careful
Use a conversational style	Friendly and confident
Speak at a moderate pace	In control; sensitive to others
Speak moderately loudly	Confident in what you are saying
Think first about what to say before you speak	Competent; wanting to be accurate
Sit up straight and make eye contact	Self-assured; secure; confident

Use the tables to verify your own experience in listening to others speak. What cues do you use to assess someone's credibility and believability? What behaviors are positive signals for you, and which detract from the person's positive impression? Judges, jurors, and attorneys are people who read others much like you do. You will learn in this book to become more sensitive to your own non-verbal cues and interpersonal messages that are being picked up by attorneys and jurors.

The Importance of Relying on Yourself

Public speaking is a very stressful event for most people. Having to answer questions that are being asked by someone with a great deal of education, who is articulate and obviously intelligent, and who knows the law, is a frightening situation no matter who you are—truck driver, corporate executive, nurse, salesman, or bank teller. No one looks forward to it, and nearly everyone dreads it.

What you know, that your attorney may not know, is that you as a person—whether you are a supervisor, a family member, a homeowner, a survivor of a bad childhood, an athlete, a disabled vet, a cancer survivor, a single parent—can get past the fear and give 100 percent of your effort. You know what is at stake. You know how strong you can be. You know how you have coped with events and situations that, in retrospect, were even more challenging. Answering questions at a deposition or giving testimony at a trial may be nerve-wracking and scary, but you can do it. Remember that no one knows more about your experience, your knowledge of events, or what you have to say at a deposition or at trial than you do. Only you know how motivated, how strong, and how capable you are, and you will bring those qualities to your job as a witness. You will learn in this book how to make the most of your strengths and manage many of your fears.

Managing Your Expectations and Emotions

Few people enjoy getting involved in a legal process, whether you are the party bringing the lawsuit or the party defending yourself against legal claims. It is an imposition on your time, it can be very stressful, and the potential outcome can be extremely significant in your life. One of your most important goals in the process is to manage your expectations and the emotions that your involvement may raise. While you may not be able to control the events involved in a legal entanglement—that is the job of the attorney—you can manage your emotional reactions.

You may be required to answer questions that not only tax your memory, but also reveal embarrassing, sensitive, private, or incriminating information. During the questioning process, your emotions can run the gamut—feelings of betrayal, disbelief, anger, resentment, fear, embarrassment, anxiety, annoyance, or mistrust. Your emotions can wax and wane as time passes between the various legal steps. Feelings of stark terror one month can be replaced by unrealistic optimism the next. Indifference at an initial meeting can transform into extreme tension as the deposition or trial nears. This is referred to as the "roller coaster of litigation," and for some people, it has the same visceral effect. This is to be expected.

The stress of an unfortunate incident, followed by a legal entanglement, is an emotional one-two punch. The resurgence of unpleasant memories during your witness-preparation session or when being questioned in a legal proceeding can open deep psychological wounds. This, too, should be expected. Remember there is life after a lawsuit and the legal proceedings will eventually be completed so that emotional healing can begin.

It is important for your attorney to know how you feel and what is causing you the most stress, but be careful not to misdirect toward your own attorney strong negative emotions you may be feeling toward the opposing party. Remember that your attorney is on your side.

Managing Anxiety

No matter how well prepared you are to give testimony at a deposition, hearing, or trial, you will be nervous. Some anxiety will actually be beneficial to you, as a managed level of stress is known to help us perform at our best. And it is unlikely you will give perfect answers to every question. You may even stumble verbally and misspeak from time to time. This, too, is to be expected. Even experienced expert witnesses sometimes make errors or fail to express themselves accurately. You will not sink the ship with a few careless words or the failure to include some item of information. All you can do is listen carefully, speak honestly, and stay focused. The rest is up to your attorney.

While a certain level of nervousness is expected, overwhelming fear is much more serious and can affect your performance negatively. Stage fright or performance anxiety is acute, often debilitating nervousness associated with having to speak or perform in front of others. It is a common reaction and many people suffer from it, but signs of extreme nervousness can be taken by a jury to indicate lying or evasiveness. Even ordinary shyness can be misread as deception.

Controlling anxiety and nervousness is essential, but not easy. However, there are ways that may be effective for you, at least in the short run. The following are some strategies that have worked for others.

Some Ways to Cope with Excessive Nervousness

• Be prepared. Do your homework and focus on information that you recall. Part of stage fright is fear you will not remember what you wish to say. Refreshing your memory will help diminish this fear.

• Reduce the significance of the questioner by imagining him or her doing ordinary things—mowing their lawn, hauling garbage. This helps to temper the imagined power we have invested in them, which contributes to our anxiety.

• Stop thinking about and imagining negative outcomes. A negative outcome is always possible, but worrying about it beforehand is a waste of energy. Practice what we call "conservation of worry." That is, don't waste worry time on events that may not happen or are completely out of your control.

• Focus your attention on the present, not on possible negative outcomes further down the road. Take it one question at a time instead of anticipating what you expect to happen later. Remember that nothing catastrophic is likely to happen.

• Put it in perspective. See the process as insignificant in relation to the totality of your life. Remind yourself that you have faced and overcome much more challenging events in your life.

• Focus on the positive aspects of the process. At the very least, giving your testimony means the legal process is moving toward resolution so you can put it behind you.

• Never underestimate the power of deep breathing. Try this: inhale to the count of eight while pushing out your stomach, then exhale to the count of ten. Do this at least six times. Amazing, isn't it?

CHAPTER 2

SOME BASICS ABOUT THE LITIGATION PROCESS

In this chapter we will cover the basics a witness needs to know about the litigation process. While no one expects you to become a lawyer overnight, having a basic understanding of legal terms and the basic steps in a litigation process will help relieve some of your anxiety about the unknown. Think of it as a class in Litigation Basics.

Civil versus Criminal Trials

There are two basic kinds of cases: civil and criminal. Most of the trials portrayed on television are criminal cases; the TV series *Damages* deals with civil lawsuits. Although criminal and civil disputes are both called legal cases in the court of law, and generally follow the same trial process, there are some distinct differences. Charges in criminal cases relate to specific laws the person is accused of breaking, and are brought by the government, not the victim. The goal in criminal trials is to determine guilt or innocence, and if the person is found guilty, to impose a sentence, i.e., punishment. Civil lawsuits, on the other hand, pertain to the rights and duties of people involved in contracts, torts (a civil wrong or injury), and other private rights. Civil claims are typically brought by an individual or organization against another individual or organization. Tort lawsuits are generally aimed at determining whether someone has been negligent, and if so, if the negligence resulted in injury or loss to another person or organization. If negligence is proven, the party bringing the lawsuit is usually awarded money compensation for harms and losses. Guilt or innocence does not apply in civil cases, only in criminal ones.

There are many kinds of civil lawsuits: personal injury, medical negligence, business disputes, employment discrimination, wrongful death, and many others. You may recall that the O. J. Simpson case involved both a criminal trial (to determine guilt or innocence) and a civil tort lawsuit (to determine liability and money damages). Mr. Simpson was found not guilty in the criminal trial, but was held liable for millions of dollars in compensatory damages in the civil lawsuit. The difference in the outcome could have been due to the difference in the burden of proof: criminal cases require the jury to reach a unanimous verdict beyond a reasonable doubt while civil lawsuits require some type of majority verdict (6 of 8, 10 of 12, etc.) based on a preponderance of the evidence. There are other differences between criminal and civil lawsuits, and your attorney is the best person to consult if you wish to know more detail.

Who's Who

If you are involved in a civil lawsuit as the person bringing the lawsuit, you are the *plaintiff*, and your attorney is plaintiff's counsel, also called the plaintiff's attorney. If you are defending against claims made by a plaintiff, you are the *defendant*, and your attorney is defense counsel or the defense attorney. If you are named specifically in the lawsuit, you are a *named party*. If you are not a named party (for example, your employer is actually the named defendant), you may be giving testimony as a *fact witness*, meaning you are not a defendant, but you know certain facts relevant to the case. You may also be asked to give testimony as an *expert witness*. Expert witnesses are people with specialized knowledge and/or experience, and they are typically paid for their time to offer independent expert opinions during a trial.

If you are involved in a criminal matter, the entity bringing the charges is the federal, state, or local government and the attorney representing the government is the prosecuting attorney, or simply the *prosecutor*. If you are defending against the charges, you are the defendant, and your attorney is either a court-appointed attorney or a defense attorney you have hired privately.

To avoid redundancy, we will often refer simply to "opposing counsel" as the attorney representing the other side of your case. When we refer to "plaintiff's attorney," you should assume that if it is a criminal matter, we mean the prosecutor.

Basic Steps in a Lawsuit

In general, all trials, whether criminal or civil, follow some basic steps. These steps may take months to complete, or they could require years. Civil cases usually extend over a longer period of time than do criminal matters, as people charged with crimes are assured a speedy trial.

Once a case has been officially filed, and a judge and trial date assigned, the attorneys on both sides engage in what is called "discovery." During this time, attorneys are investigating, gathering information, talking with experts, getting evidence and exhibits together, and generally preparing for the trial phase of the case. If you are required to give a deposition (discussed in the following chapter), this will take place during the discovery phase.

Occasionally in civil cases, the parties may agree to settle their dispute outside of a court setting. They may engage a mediator, or they may submit their controversy to an arbitrator who acts like a judge and decides the case. If this does not occur, the issues will be settled in a court of law by a panel of jurors. Unlike television portrayals of trials that are often completed in an hour, most courtroom proceedings require substantial time, anywhere from a day or two for a simple case, or up to many months for complex litigation.

CHAPTER 3

ABOUT DEPOSITIONS

In a civil case (and under limited circumstances in a criminal case), depositions are usually completed in preparation for the trial. A deposition is a statement of a witness made under oath, taken in question-and-answer format as it would be in court. It is taken by the opposing party's attorney. The proceedings are recorded by an authorized officer, such as a court reporter or stenographer. In a civil case, most of the key witnesses are deposed, and each is done individually.

What a Deposition Is

A deposition is the opposing party's opportunity to question you prior to trial about any facts you know or records you authored that are relevant to the lawsuit. It is taken during the discovery phase of a lawsuit. It usually occurs months and even years before a lawsuit or case goes to trial. Although a deposition is conducted by the opposing party's attorney, your attorney will be with you.

Few people are familiar with the deposition process because depositions are not included in televised courtroom dramas, either real or enacted. Since depositions often include very broad questioning, not all responses given by a witness may be admissible at trial. Therefore, even watching a real-life trial (such as in the reality television series, *In Session*) rarely reveals all that can be asked in a deposition.

Your Attorney's Role

Although your attorney will accompany you to your deposition, your attorney cannot help you answer questions—you must answer each question on your own. Your attorney's role is to ensure the court's rules are followed, to ensure the questions asked are in proper form, to make objections for the record, and to provide emotional support to you. You will be able to consult privately with your attorney during breaks, but not during the questioning (except in very rare circumstances). It is unlikely your attorney will ask any questions at your deposition, unless something needs clarification. If that is the case, your attorney will ask you a few questions at the end.

The Purpose of a Deposition

A deposition is a one-sided process—it is taken so the opposing party can learn what you know before you give testimony at trial. It also gives opposing counsel an opportunity to make certain assessments of you, and to achieve other purposes that the attorney hopes will strengthen his or her case. The following table summarizes some of the main goals of the attorney who has requested your deposition. Not all of these purposes may apply in your specific case.

Reasons for Opposing Counsel to Take Your Deposition

- Learn what you know about the events at issue.

- Commit you to statements under oath that cannot be easily changed later.

- Obtain from you certain admissions, confessions, declarations, or concessions that opposing counsel hopes will help his or her case.

- Look for ways to get you to make statements that conflict with those of other witnesses.

- Find out if you have hot buttons that will trigger anger, defensiveness, or other negative emotions that will hurt your effectiveness or believability.

- Determine if you can be easily manipulated or intimidated through skillful questioning into saying something inaccurate or not completely truthful.

- Gain information from you that may help discover facts previously unknown.

- Assess your ability to listen, recall, and give accurate and effective testimony.

- Assess your credibility and juror appeal—whether jurors will like you, feel sympathy for you, believe you, criticize your demeanor, or exercise certain prejudices against you because of how you present yourself, speak, act, and communicate.

While it may feel uncomfortable or inconvenient to give a deposition, remember that your attorney will be deposing witnesses on the other side as part of the discovery process in your case also. The deposition process is a normal part of legal proceedings and you should not view it as merely an opportunity to harass or intimidate you.

The purpose of taking a deposition in a criminal case is usually different from a civil case. In civil cases, depositions are normally taken to discover information that's relevant to the case. In criminal cases, on the other hand, depositions are normally taken to preserve testimony from a witness who may not be available for trial. (Note that preservation depositions may also be taken in civil matters.) A deposition is not meant as a discovery device in a criminal matter.

What a Deposition Is NOT

Contrary to what most people assume, the deposition is NOT the place to tell your complete story or to try to convince opposing counsel to drop the case. Many witnesses believe (or hope) that if they simply tell everything they know and give a solid explanation of why things happened as they did, the opposing party will realize they don't have a strong case and will fold up their tent and drop the lawsuit. This rarely, if ever, happens. Attempts to tell your complete story at a deposition will give opposing counsel more information that could be used against you. Just answer the questions in a succinct and focused manner. Nothing more and nothing less. In fact, you may leave your deposition disappointed that the attorney did not ask questions you expected to be asked, or that you considered important but were bypassed. Do not do opposing counsel's job by anticipating what the attorney wants to know or providing information outside the specific questions being asked.

Despite your desire to make it so, a deposition is NOT a conversation. It is a very precise and in many ways unnatural question-and-answer session. The questions will be asked in an unfamiliar environment, by a stranger, with considerable formality, in the language of lawyer-speak, with all eyes on you. There is no way to sugarcoat this—it is likely to make you quite nervous. Tempting as it is to try to relax by being personable and chatty, this is a very bad strategy. Consider the following exchange:

> Q. *I notice that you seem a little distracted. Are you on medication today?*
>
> A. *No, no medications.*
>
> Q. *I only ask that question because it is important that you and I can have a conversation today and understand each other.*

Note that opposing counsel is attempting to persuade the witness that the deposition is merely a conversation, such that friends might have. It may be designed to put you in a more relaxed and less guarded frame of mind. Don't fall for this. Keep your guard up. Opposing counsel is not your friend. Remember that he or she works for the other side and is committed to doing the best possible job for his or her client.

The deposition is NOT the place to demonstrate how cooperative you can be, how hard you are trying to please the attorney, or how helpful you are by nature. It is not the place to display your personality traits, whether they include being warm and outgoing, or sullen and argumentative. Your purpose at deposition is not to convince the opposing attorney that you are a nice (or a fearsome) person, but rather to merely answer questions. Leave your social skills and your debating abilities out of it.

A deposition is NOT the place to vent your anger, frustration, fear, or disappointment about being involved in legal proceedings. Negative emotions will have no real effect on the deposing attorney, and they will only interfere with your purposes. Check your negative baggage at the door. If necessary you can reclaim it when you leave the deposition. You may also feel resentment if you are asked questions of a personal or sensitive nature, if you are asked to reveal personal secrets, or if you are asked about events that are embarrassing or humiliating. Your attorney may have grounds to object to some of these kinds of questions, but if the information is relevant to the case, you will likely have to answer the questions. It is best to sit up to the table and face them head-on, with honesty and candor. Anything less will be seen as weaseling and your credibility will suffer.

Notorious past attempts at sidestepping embarrassing questions in prominent trials proved to merely prolong the legal wrangling. For example, you may recall the problems of ex-president Bill Clinton (who quibbled about his relationship with Monica Lewinsky), Mark Fuhrman (who quibbled about his use of racially prejudicial terms), or the Enron executives (who tried to dodge questions regarding financial maneuvers). Weaseling and sidestepping are usually transparent and serve only to whet the appetite of an aggressive attorney who will jump at the chance to expose your evasiveness.

CHAPTER 4

GIVING A DEPOSITION

Giving a deposition can be worrisome, regardless of your background, profession, experience with the legal process, or the extent of your involvement in the case or criminal proceeding. Ask any attorney who has been deposed and they will likely admit that even being very familiar with the process does not completely eliminate the anxiety factor.

Communication in a deposition is not like any other form of communication you have had or will likely have again in the future. You will be asked questions in a formal setting, with considerable formality, and in the language of attorneys. You will be asked precise questions that you are not accustomed to answering in this format. Remember that a deposition is a very unusual mode of communication, so expect it to be somewhat uncomfortable and unfamiliar.

The Setting

Your deposition will most likely take place in a conference room at your attorney's office. However, it could also be taken at opposing counsel's office, your workplace, a court stenography office, a teleconferencing center, a jail or incarceration facility, or in your home if you are disabled or otherwise unable to travel. Convenience for those attending is typically the most important factor, but some attorneys have been known to jockey for a home court advantage by insisting the deposition be held in their offices.

In attendance will be your attorney, the opposing party's attorney (who will be asking the questions), and the court stenographer, who will be recording everything that is said. There may also be a videographer. The person or persons named in the lawsuit have a right to attend your deposition, and sometimes they do. Insurance claims representatives also have the right to attend. Ask your attorney who will be there so you know what to expect.

If you are one of several plaintiffs or defendants, attorneys representing the other parties may also attend your deposition, either in person or by teleconference, and they may also ask you questions when the deposing attorney has finished. Typically, these questions will focus on clarifying any answers you have given involving their clients.

Everyone in attendance will introduce themselves. You will likely be seated at the head of the table, with others seated around. If your deposition is being videotaped, the camera operator may position you. You will be sworn in, just as if you were in court. The questioning attorney will then give you some basic rules that you will be expected to follow. Typical instructions include:

- Speak up so the stenographer is certain to hear you.

- Wait until a question is complete before starting to answer it. This helps the stenographer.

- If you don't understand a question, say so. If you answer a question, it is assumed that you understood it, and you cannot later claim your answer was based on a misunderstanding of the question.

- Answer in words, not uh-huh, nah, yup, yeah, a nod, or a shoulder shrug. The stenographer can only record words, not body language.

- You may take a break when you need one, but not while a question is pending.

- Typically, you may not consult with your attorney before answering a question.

As soon as you have agreed to these rules, the deposing attorney (the attorney who made the request to take your deposition) will begin the questioning.

If Your Deposition Is to Be Video-Recorded

It is not uncommon in today's legal environment for attorneys to video-record depositions. This is typically done for several reasons:

- Video-recording captures not only what you say, but your demeanor—nervous habits, facial expressions, body language, long pauses, etc. Segments of your video-recorded deposition could be shown to jurors at trial if opposing counsel thinks your body language or demeanor indicates you are not telling the truth.

- Opposing counsel may presume that the presence of the camera will increase the pressure you experience, heighten your nervousness, and keep you from thinking clearly.

- Opposing counsel may wish to show segments of your video-recorded deposition to an expert, a trial consultant, or to mock jurors in order to obtain opinions about the potential impact of your testimony before the case goes to trial.

Most people do not like to be video-recorded, believe they make a poor appearance on video, or simply resent the additional pressure. Do not worry about video-recording. The camera will quickly fade out of consciousness at your deposition as you become engaged in the process and forget about its presence. In any event, it is unlikely your attorney can oppose the video-recording of your deposition unless timely notice is required by opposing counsel and such notice was not given.

Although it is a general rule to keep your deposition answers very succinct, keep in mind that if your deposition is being video-recorded, your answers could be played to jurors during a trial. In that case, very short answers could be interpreted as a sign that you are being dishonest or that you are withholding information. If your deposition is video-recorded, your attorney may suggest that you formulate more complete answers than you might ordinarily give. Remember that if your deposition is being video-recorded, your audience is actually a jury panel, not the attorneys.

Sequence of Questioning in a Deposition

The sequence in which questions are asked in a deposition varies considerably, depending on the attorney's style and goals. Some attorneys begin a deposition by asking introductory questions such as who you are, where you live, your educational background, your work history, and other general questions. This provides an opportunity for both the witness and the attorney to get past the initial jitters and get into the question-and-answer (Q&A) mode. Only later will the attorney move into the issues central to the lawsuit.

There is no guarantee, however, that the attorney taking your deposition will follow this pattern. He or she could begin your deposition by asking the most difficult or challenging questions at the beginning of the session. Here are some examples of questions that the witnesses likely did not anticipate being asked at the very beginning of a deposition.

Examples of Difficult or Unexpected Opening Questions

Q: *Exactly how fast were you speeding when you crashed into my client's car, causing the head injuries from which she later died, and making orphans of her children?*

Q: *Why are you suing my client? What do you hope to gain by this lawsuit?*

Q: *Tell me everything that has gone wrong with your life since the accident.*

Q: *How do you sleep at night knowing you ruined my client's future?*

Q: *How many other surgeries like the one you performed on my client have you botched?*

Q: *Let's see. This is your fourth failed marriage over the past twenty years, isn't it?*

Q. *How soon after your breakup with Melissa did you start formulating your plan to begin stalking her?*

These kinds of questions are designed to throw you off your guard or spike your nervousness. Be prepared for the most difficult questions you are likely to be asked to be presented in the first five minutes of your deposition. Then you will be prepared regardless of where the attorney begins questioning.

How Objections Will Be Handled

At times during your deposition, your attorney may object to a question you have been asked. The question may be objectionable for various reasons, but do not concern yourself with the legal reasons. You need to do only one thing—stop talking. If a judge were present, the judge would rule on the objection—either sustained (approved) or overruled (not approved). Since there is no judge present at a deposition, there can be no ruling on an objection. However, your attorney must make an objection for the record so it can be ruled on by a judge if the same question is asked later in court.

In many states, attorneys are not allowed to make "speaking objections." This means the attorney is not allowed to indicate the reason for the objection. For example, your attorney cannot say, "I object to the question because that information was not known to my client until after the incident occurred." When speaking objections are not allowed, your attorney will be restricted to only a few statements, such as:

- "I object. Asked and answered." (This means the attorney feels you have given a good answer and opposing counsel should not ask it again.)

- "I object to the form of the question." (This means your attorney considers it a poor question or a question that is not properly stated.)

- "I object. Assumes facts not in evidence." (This means the questioner has not laid the proper foundation for the question, you lack the knowledge or expertise to answer it, and/or it could be a trick question.)

- "I object. The question is compound." (This means there are several questions included in a single question and opposing counsel must ask only one at a time.)

- "I object. Your question invades attorney-client privilege." (Expect your attorney to instruct you not to answer this question.)

After your attorney has made the objection, s/he may instruct you to "go ahead and answer if you can" (except for a question that invades attorney-client confidentiality). If you recall the question exactly as asked, answer it. If you cannot, ask for the question to be repeated. Then answer it, but only if you are able. Keep in mind that objections are made for legal reasons and are not necessarily intended to hint at the appropriate answer. However, the very nature of the objection should provide clues about your attorney's concerns, so be certain to pay attention to objections that are voiced.

How Long a Deposition Lasts

The length of a deposition varies considerably, depending upon your role in the events at issue in the lawsuit. It can last from a half hour up to several days. If your role in the case is minimal, the deposition could be completed in an hour or less. If you are the plaintiff or the defendant, you can expect the deposition to require two to four hours or more. If your involvement in the case spans years, or if there are many documents and exhibits to be explained, it could take up to an entire day. On rare occasions, depositions are continued for several days. Ask the attorney how long s/he expects your deposition to last, as the deposing attorney may have requested a specific timeframe.

Each attorney also has his or her own style and pace when taking a deposition. Some are efficient and to-the-point; others take more protracted depositions. The best person to gauge the possible length of your deposition is your own attorney. Your attorney is likely to have had prior experience with the opposing party's attorney and can advise you about the style and demeanor you can expect during the deposition. On occasion, your attorney may not know who is conducting the deposition, as it might be another attorney in the opposing law firm.

In rare instances, you may be asked to give a second deposition. This typically occurs when new facts come to light about which you may have knowledge, but were not known at the time of your original deposition. In such a situation, you typically can only be asked about the new information, so the deposition is likely to be shorter and more to the point.

Every Word Is Permanently Recorded

Not every legal proceeding includes the transcription of everything said by everyone in attendance. However, every word spoken at a deposition is taken down by a court stenographer and transcribed into a written document, and/or recorded on video. For this reason, everything you say at a deposition must be carefully considered before it is uttered. There can be no editing later. Although your attorney may ask you to read the written transcript to ensure its accuracy, you cannot make substantive changes unless your answer was transcribed incorrectly or the stenographer did not hear accurately what was said. In other words, corrections are allowed, but not alterations of testimony.

Taking Breaks

You may have the endurance of a racecar driver, but breaks during your deposition are important. Take at least one break each hour. If your attorney does not suggest one, ask for one. You may not take a break while a question is pending, for obvious reasons. Breaks help you clear your thoughts and allow you to get some air or a drink of water, and to stretch. This is important, so don't forget to insist on breaks. If your attorney asks for a break, take it. S/he may require a break to speak to you about something. Be careful about making comments off the record, however, because opposing counsel will likely ask you about them when back on the record.

Don't Offer to Supply Documents

You should not conduct any independent investigations or research (such as going to the site of an accident and making your own measurements, doing an on-line search on a topic, or conducting a literature search) without first consulting your attorney. You may be asked in a deposition about your findings of such investigations.

If asked by opposing counsel to supply him or her with certain documents (such as a company report, medical records, your work history resume, personal journal or records, etc.), it is best to reply, "I can provide those [if you able to do so] through my attorney." Never supply opposing counsel directly with any materials that have not first been examined by your attorney. Nor should you ever spontaneously offer to provide documents, such as in the following exchange from an actual deposition: "The literature supports my position. I have done some investigation of the expert opinions on this issue, and to prove my point, I can supply you with copies of those articles." This offer not only provided opposing counsel with information that could be subsequently refuted, it required considerable time on the part of the witness to assemble it. Don't do opposing counsel's work for him or her.

CHAPTER 5

TESTIFYING AT TRIAL

Preparing to go to court raises many emotions—anticipation, anxiety about testifying, worry about the outcome, and concerns about what you should and should not do. Who will be there? What happens first? What should I wear? Where will I sit? When will I be called? Should I look at the jurors when I answer questions? If you are going to trial for the first time, this chapter will answer many of those questions. If a courtroom is already familiar to you, this chapter may clear up some misconceptions.

The Basic Setup

In addition to the judge, trials are typically staffed with a minimum of a court stenographer (unless the trial is being audio-recorded), a court clerk, and a bailiff or jury administrator. In criminal trials, the prosecutor and his or her assistant is seated at one table, the criminal defendant and his or her attorney at another. In a civil case, the plaintiff (or a representative) and the defendant are seated at tables with their attorneys, unless health or disability prevents attendance. Other attorneys from the law offices and/or legal assistants may also be seated at the tables. If there are multiple parties on either side, there will be additional attorneys and parties present. There may be court observers, members of the families of the parties involved, or media representatives in the gallery (the bench seats behind the attorney tables). Unless your case is media-worthy, it is unlikely any reporters will attend.

Trials are typically conducted from 9:00 AM to 4:30 PM, with a midmorning break, an hour and half for lunch, and a midafternoon break.

This varies widely, however, from judge to judge. In many jurisdictions, court is held only four days of the week, enabling judges to deal with other matters on the fifth day. Be certain to ask the attorney about the schedule. Be patient if the judge starts the day earlier or later than 9:00 AM, or goes past 4:30 or even 5:00 PM. This may be necessary to accommodate jurors and/or witnesses. Judges may also have other court matters and emergencies that require attention before court can begin.

While judges may not always start court on time, they expect attorneys and parties to mind the clock. Being late for court is not acceptable. Allow plenty of time to get to the courthouse on time, find parking, get through security, and locate the courtroom. Courthouses, like airports, maintain strict security, and you will be required to pass through a security checkpoint and metal detector. Federal courthouses also require photographic identification, so do not forget to bring yours.

If you are a party to the lawsuit (plaintiff or defendant), your attorney will likely require you to attend court every day. If you are a fact or an expert witness, the attorney will notify you of the date and estimated time at which you will be expected to appear.

What to Ask the Attorney

If you are unfamiliar with the trial process, ask the attorney to explain the general steps and procedures that will be followed during the trial. This will help reduce the unknowns and help you understand when during the trial your testimony will be needed. You may ask the attorney to explain who specifically will be in attendance at trial, who will be asking questions and in what sequence, and how long you should expect to be on the stand. Ask the attorney to clarify your role and responsibilities during the trial process so you will know where your testimony fits into the overall trial plan. Inquire if there is anything the attorney is expecting you to bring to trial (such as office records, samples, demonstrative aids, etc.).

If you are new to the litigation process, ask your attorney to take you to the courtroom where you will be testifying, especially if you are a party in the case. If you have never observed or participated in a live court proceeding, ask about observing a different trial before yours, preferably with the same judge. Familiarity can ease anxiety about the unknown.

Steps in a Trial

If you have never before been a party or a witness at a trial, ask your attorney to explain the typical steps. The following simplified explanation of the basic steps should be helpful. Remember that not all types of legal proceedings include all of these steps.

Basic Steps in a Trial

1. Arguing of motions related to admissibility of testimony and evidence (and other issues) without a jury present.

2. Jury pool is brought to the courtroom.

3. Introduction of the parties and their attorneys; a brief statement of the case by the judge.

4. Questioning of the jury pool by the judge and the attorneys (called *voir dire*).

5. Jury selection and seating of the jury panel (usually eight to twelve people).

6. Opening statement made by each side, beginning with plaintiff's attorney, to outline the evidence each attorney intends to present, and his or her theory of the case (usually about one hour per side).

7. Plaintiff's or prosecutor's entire case is presented, including claims, evidence, and witness testimony; defense allowed to cross-examine plaintiff's or prosecutor's witnesses.

8. Defense's entire case is presented; plaintiff or prosecutor allowed to cross-examine the defense's witnesses.

9. Possible rebuttal arguments by plaintiff's counsel.

10. Closing argument made by each side, beginning with plaintiff's attorney, to summarize the evidence and key arguments that were presented (usually about one hour per side).

11. Jury instructions by the judge to the jury panel (some preliminary instructions may be given at the start of the trial; jury instructions given before closing arguments in some states).

12. Jury deliberations, using a Verdict Form listing the questions the jury is to decide.

13. Verdict delivered by the jury or judge.

14. Sentencing (if appropriate, and in criminal trials only).

If your case does not involve a jury (for example, a hearing or a bench trial in which a judge alone decides the outcome), some steps obviously will be omitted. If you are a party in the case, you will likely be present for all steps, depending upon what your attorney decides is best. If you are a fact or expert witness, you will be required to be present only when your testimony is needed. In fact, in most but not all trials, witnesses who are not parties are excluded from the courtroom until after they have given their testimony.

When You Will Be Called Upon

It is up to your attorney to decide where in the trial your testimony will be required. You may not necessarily be the first witness called to the stand. Unless you are a named party in the case (that is, either a plaintiff or a defendant), you will not be called to the courtroom until it is time for you to take the stand. After you have given your testimony, you may remain in the courtroom, but you are not allowed in the courtroom until then. If you are a named party, you will likely be seated at counsel table with your attorney for the entire trial. If that is the case, you will have the opportunity to observe opposing counsel's questioning style, how other witnesses respond, and jurors' reactions as witnesses respond to questions.

On occasion, plaintiff's counsel may choose to call a defense witness during the plaintiff's case. If this happens to you, then you are considered an "adverse" (meaning opposing) witness. If you are called adversely, you will be questioned first by the plaintiff's attorney, and your attorney may or may not ask you questions when plaintiff's counsel is finished. Your attorney may wish to wait until the defense starts its case so you can give more complete testimony. Calling a witness adversely is a strategy often used when opposing counsel expects you to make a poor witness or to give testimony damaging to your case. Being called adversely is a special condition and you should ask your attorney about the probability of this occurring. As you can imagine, it presents special challenges that will require extra guidance from your attorney.

If you are a defendant in a criminal case, you have a constitutional right (Fifth Amendment) not to be forced to testify against yourself. In fact, a witness can almost always refuse to answer a question on the grounds that the answer could be incriminating. People can be reluctant to exercise this right because of how it may be viewed by jurors. To jurors, "pleading the Fifth" can sometimes signal inherent guilt or the fear of having guilt exposed through cross-examination. They wonder, "If the defendant is really innocent, why doesn't s/he testify and tell his or her side of the story?" However, the decision about whether or not to take the stand in your own defense is an important decision that can be made by you and your attorney only after careful consideration of many factors.

Physical Appearance Is Very Important

Just as you were advised to do for your deposition, it is very important to look credible by paying attention to your personal appearance and demeanor when going to trial. Make certain you are well-groomed, dressed in clean, pressed clothes, and wearing appropriate shoes. This will make a good impression and will show respect for the court and jury members. Showing up in a T-shirt and old Levis will not impress anyone. Nor is it necessary to show jurors how "needy" you are, or how you are suffering financially, by dressing in shabby clothing. Look and act respectable and responsible if you wish to gain the respect of the jurors.

If you are a professional, look and act like one. Professional men should avoid wearing a somber black suit and white shirt. Even though it may feel like it at times, you are not attending a funeral and need not dress for one. If you have been advised to wear a suit and tie, make it a navy blue, brown, or gray suit, with a light blue or cream-colored shirt and a conservative tie with a simple pattern. If you are not the suit-and-tie type, wear dress slacks and a conservative shirt, dress shoes, and a sweater if the weather is cold. A suit coat and tie is not necessary unless that is what you normally wear to work.

Long hair on males is still considered a symbol of rebelliousness or nonconformity, and it makes a poor impression on most jurors. Consider having it cut and re-grow it after the trial. If you wear a beard and/or mustache, make certain it is neatly trimmed. If you are not very attached to it, consider shaving it off. If it hides a facial feature about which you are self-conscious, leave it on. Men who wear an open-collar shirt should not wear neck chains or necklaces. The point is to appear mainstream and conservative. Drawing attention to your appearance or clothing pulls attention away from your testimony.

Women should tone down makeup, avoid flashy and dangling jewelry, and wear conservative clothing. It is not necessary to look like a nerdy librarian, but conservative dress and appearance is always the preferred look. Expensive jewelry could signal jurors that you are already wealthy, so leave it at home. Do not arrive in court with stiletto heels, fur trims, bleached blond hair with black roots, pink and orange hair extensions, and heavy colored eye shadow. Avoid anything low-cut, brightly colored, covered in ruffles, too tight, too short, or too sheer. You will not sway male jurors by appearing sexy or alluring; you will most likely just destroy your credibility with female jurors.

If you have long hair, get it cut or tie it back. Make certain your hair is clean and neat. If you have tattoos, cover them. If you have facial piercings, take out the jewelry. If you have a statement to make about your appearance, make it before or after your appearance in court. Like it or not, mainstream America doubts the credibility of parties and witnesses who appear in court to be out of the mainstream. If you want jurors to identify and sympathize with your case, it is important that you look and act like them.

Be on your best behavior at all times. Watch your attitude and demeanor. Acting flippant, arrogant, hostile, nasty, or mean-spirited will not help your case; it can only hurt it. You will have very definite feelings about your involvement in a legal entanglement, but the courtroom is no place to vent those feelings.

Don't use alcohol, drugs, or medications that could affect your behavior before you are scheduled to testify. If you are taking medications that might affect your ability to concentrate or testify, discuss this with your attorney well in advance. You will want to consult with the prescribing physician before stopping any prescribed medications.

Don't chew tobacco or gum while testifying. You will not be allowed to bring food or drink, other than water, into the courtroom. Be certain to turn off your cell phone, and do not send or read text messages while seated at counsel table. Wait until a break to turn your phone back on and do so only after the jury has left the courtroom.

Taking and Leaving the Stand

When called to the stand, walk confidently to the witness box. If you act as though you are walking to the gallows, jurors may assume you are anticipating failure. Stand up straight, hold your head up, and sit up straight in the witness chair. Your posture and demeanor should reflect confidence, not defeat.

After you are sworn in by court personnel, sit down and position your chair with a slight angle toward the jury box. This will make it easier to look at the jurors when answering questions so you will not have to twist your head as though watching a tennis match. Sit up in the chair and plant your feet on the floor to prevent unconscious swiveling or rocking when you get nervous. You will likely have a small bench in front of you with a microphone. Move the microphone closer to you if necessary, but never lean over and talk into the microphone. This is what mobsters and crooked politicians do in television shows.

Next, look at the jurors and acknowledge them by smiling or nodding your head at them. You may even feel comfortable enough to say, "Good morning" or "Good afternoon," but that is all you can say to them directly. Remember that jurors are the most important people in the courtroom because they are the ones who will deliberate and decide on your case—not the judge, not the attorneys, only the people in the jury box. They deserve your respect and attention.

When leaving the stand, walk with the same confidence as when you took it. Even if you feel battered and tired, leave the witness box as if you have been the most effective witness of the day. However, do not give the attorney (or the jurors) a thumbs-up, a high-five, or a victory sign. Remember that while you should feel good about your testimony and performance, you have not yet won the battle.

Interactions with Attorneys and Jurors

It is important to treat the opposing attorney with the same courtesy you would show your own attorney, the judge, or the jurors. By remaining respectful, patient, and calm during difficult questioning by opposing counsel, you give jurors the impression that you have nothing to hide and no reason to become angry or defensive. You don't want to appear as one person when your own attorney is questioning you (calm, patient, confident, respectful) and another when opposing counsel is questioning you (defensive, argumentative, angry, insolent). Jurors will wonder which personality is the real you. Although no one expects you to be warm and friendly to opposing counsel, strong negative emotion of any kind, sarcasm, and/or open hostility in the courtroom makes jurors uncomfortable. Jurors tend to discount testimony from witnesses who give off a negative vibe.

At a jury trial, you are speaking to jurors, not to attorneys or the presiding judge. Eye contact with jurors is important because this is how we often judge someone's honesty—by their willingness to look us in the eye. However, if you are uncomfortable making eye contact with jurors, don't force it. If jurors get the impression you are looking at them merely in order to influence or persuade them, the effort will be transparent and you risk alienating them. It may appear you have been coached by your attorney to give them eye contact even though it makes you uncomfortable.

Some attorneys deliberately try to force your attention away from jurors by locking in your eye contact and asking short, closed-end questions that require a very short answer—preferably a simple "yes" or "no." Your attorney, however, will most likely take a position in the courtroom that will enable you to look at both the attorney and the jurors—usually at the far corner of the jury box. If courtroom rules require attorneys to remain at a podium when questioning witnesses, do the best you can to give jurors as much eye contact as is comfortable for you. Avoid twisting your head back and forth as if watching a tennis match. This will look staged.

Star-Witness and Sinker-Witness Complexes

Some people develop a sense of exaggerated self-importance, referred to by several witness experts as the "star-witness fantasy." That is, the witness comes to believe that his or her testimony, along with personal charisma and persuasiveness, will make or break the case. The attitude implies, "Once the jurors hear what I have to say, it will be open-and-shut." This can happen inadvertently, especially when a witness is aware of only one piece of a complex trial strategy, or when a person has an exaggerated sense of self-importance to begin with.

The other side of the star-witness fantasy is the "sinker-witness complex." In this scenario, the witness becomes convinced that his or her testimony is so sensitive or so damaging that as soon as jurors hear it, the ship will be sunk and the case will be lost. The belief is, "Once the jurors hear what I have to say, we won't stand a chance." Again, this complex can stem from a lack of awareness about the entirety of the case and the role to be played by other witnesses.

If you feel yourself falling victim to either witness complex, remind yourself of the reality of most trials. A case is comprised of hundreds, perhaps thousands of pieces of evidence, testimony, exhibits, arguments, motions, and documents that will factor into how the case is ultimately decided. If you burden yourself with the belief that your testimony is a pivotal point for winning or losing the case, you have tripled your anxiety quotient unnecessarily. In most cases, you are a part of the process, but not the entirety.

How to Address Opposing Counsel and the Judge

In the courtroom (and for that matter, in a deposition), it is not necessary to address opposing counsel by name or title. It is also not necessary to use the deferential title "ma'am" or "sir" unless it is your nature to do so by virtue of your upbringing. Opposing counsel may use a formal address in asking questions; for example, "Tell us, Mrs. Smith, why you did not use the north entrance to the building." However, it is not necessary to reciprocate. Just answer the question without prefacing it with a title. Remember that technically you are not answering the attorney, you are answering to the jurors (or the judge). If it is necessary to address the judge, the proper title is "Your Honor."

How Objections Will Be Handled

When objections are made in court, the judge will rule on each. The objection will be sustained (approved) or overruled (disapproved). If the objection is sustained, the witness does not answer; if the objection is overruled, the judge will direct you to answer the question. Unless you are claiming protection under the Fifth Amendment, you must answer if directed by the judge to do so, if you can give an honest and accurate answer. If you refuse to respond to a question you are capable of answering, you risk being held in contempt of court, which carries legal penalties.

Being Under Scrutiny by Jurors

If you are seated with your attorney at counsel table throughout the trial, be aware that jurors are observing you nearly all the time, not just when you are on the stand. They are observing how you interact with your attorney, your physical and emotional reactions to the testimony provided by others, how attentive or inattentive you are during the proceedings, and other aspects of your behavior. Are you falling asleep? Doodling on a pad of paper? Absently picking lint off your jacket? Furiously writing pages of notes? Jiggling your leg constantly? Jurors want to learn as much about you as possible so they can judge your personality, your motives, and your credibility. They do so by observing you throughout the trial. What does this mean for you? Simple—be on your toes at all times. Be yourself, but be your *best* self.

Courtroom Demeanor

When you are in the courtroom, your attention should be on the proceedings. Do not bring a book, newspaper, or office work to court. Dress appropriately every day, whether or not you are to be on the stand. When a witness is giving testimony, give the witness your full attention, but without any outward indication of how you are feeling about that witness's testimony. No head shaking, nodding, eye rolling, table slapping, yawning, or verbal outbursts of any kind. Jurors resent this kind of behavior and consider it rude and inappropriate. If you need to convey some information to your attorney, write it discreetly on a pad of paper, or wait for a break. Don't pull on your attorney's sleeve, lean over and whisper repeatedly (although it may be necessary occasionally), or pass the attorney a large number of notes. Sit up to the table and don't slouch as if you are bored or uninterested. Although you have legal representation, this is your case after all. Jurors expect you to be attentive and interested at all times. They try very hard to be focused and attentive, so you should also.

Avoid contact with jurors at all times outside the courtroom. They will be instructed not to interact with you in any way. Don't use the bathroom when they are using it, and be careful about running into them (literally or figuratively) in the parking lot. If you recognize a juror in a restaurant or store during the trial, make certain there is no interaction. Anything beyond "Good morning" or "Excuse me" is considered inappropriate by the Court and could be grounds for an admonishment, or perhaps even a mistrial.

Courtrooms Can Be Intimidating

For many of us, courtrooms are familiar because we see them often on television shows. But when we must physically enter one, it can be very daunting and formidable. For this reason, a visit to a courtroom (any courtroom) before trial may be wise. If feasible, sit in the witness chair in advance so you can become somewhat desensitized to the anxiety rush you will likely feel when first entering the witness box. Look at the jury box and imagine a group of people looking back at you as you speak. Imagine yourself getting comfortable in the chair. Imagine the jurors paying attention as you speak. Breathe slowly and relax.

Attorneys Can Be Intimidating

When attorneys question witnesses in a courtroom, they are usually standing while the witness is seated in a chair. This puts you automatically in a subservient position. Your submissiveness can become even more obvious if you slouch down in the chair, look away from the attorney, cross your arms or legs, or lean away from the attorney. Instead of appearing meek and deferential, sit up erect and make yourself as tall as possible. You may even try leaning slightly forward, as though you are reaching out or seeking contact.

In some venues, the attorney must remain at a podium or at counsel table when questioning witnesses in order to avoid threat or intimidation. When not prohibited, some attorneys attempt to intimidate witnesses by standing very close, leaning in, and intruding into personal space. We might characterize this as "getting in your face." The effect is often as intended—the witness feels defensive and unnerved. If this should happen, try responding in kind. That is, lean into the attorney and invade his or her personal space. Chances are he or she will back off.

CHAPTER 6

DIFFERENCES AND SIMILARITIES
IN DEPOSITIONS AND TRIAL

Being a witness at trial is quite different from answering questions at a deposition. At trial, your testimony will be considered and weighed by a trial judge or a panel of jurors. Your deposition is attended by only a handful of people, but at trial you are in the witness box, delivering your answers to a large group of people: attorneys, the opposing party and members of his or her family, jurors, court personnel, trial observers, and possibly representatives of the media. If you have given a deposition already, your testimony at trial will be compared for consistency with the statements you made at the deposition. A panel of strangers will be judging your case, and the outcome is likely final. There is much at stake.

Not only have the circumstances changed, but the process and rules for giving testimony at trial are now quite different. If you were properly prepared for your deposition, much of what you learned is not applicable at trial, and you must learn new rules. In this chapter we show you what is different between deposition and trial testimony, and what rules apply in both situations.

Key Differences Between Deposition and Trial Testimony

The differences between deposition and trial testimony are important because they dictate how you prepare, and how you answer questions. Here is a simple summary of the differences. Note that a reference to jurors or a jury includes judges, panel members, or other fact finders who will ultimately vote on the issues in your case.

A Witness *at a Deposition*:	A Witness *at Trial*:
Understands this is primarily *cross-examination* by opposing counsel; it is an opportunity to find out what you know so opposing counsel can be prepared for trial; it is unlikely one's own attorney will ask any questions unless something needs to be clarified at the end	Understands that s/he is subject to both *direct examination* by one's own attorney and *cross-examination* by opposing counsel, as well as re-direct and re-cross (meaning both attorneys get a second chance to ask follow-up questions)
Answers *only* the question asked, in a very succinct form, and does not provide unnecessary background or history	Answers questions *fully* under direct examination by his/her own attorney and as succinctly as possible under cross-examination by opposing counsel
Understands that this is *not* the place to tell one's story, but merely to answer the specific questions asked	Understands this *is* the place to tell his/her story to the jury, but it must be done in a coherent and organized fashion so as to be understood by others
Realizes that the mode of communication is *not* a conversation, but rather a specific question-and-answer format	Realizes that answers must be in a more conversational format because the audience is jurors, not attorneys
Makes eye contact primarily with the questioning attorney	Makes as much reasonable eye contact as possible with the jurors, since they are the only ones who get to decide the case at the end of the trial
Sticks to the role of answering questions and does not go outside his/her area of knowledge or expertise	Acts as an educator of jurors, rather than a plaintiff, defendant, or expert witness
Knows that his/her attorney is there primarily as an observer, to voice objections if necessary, and to ensure a proper record is made	Knows that his/her own attorney is a powerful advocate who will present his/her side of the story and actively persuade the jury to decide in one's favor

Understands that no jury (or no decision-maker) is present	Realizes a jury is present, made up of ordinary people who will be judging the evidence and testimony of witnesses in order to decide the case
Will be sworn to tell the truth by the court reporter or stenographer who is present	Will be sworn to tell the truth before giving testimony on the stand
Has been told that objections by one's own attorney will be noted for the record, but the witness will most likely have to answer all questions anyway (unless they violate attorney-client privilege)	Has been told that objections by the attorney will be ruled on by the judge; knows one should stop talking until a ruling has been made
Realizes the setting is rather informal, but the rules are still formal	Can be intimidated by the formal and solemn setting
Is aware that a court stenographer is taking down every word said by every person and a written transcript will be prepared that can be ordered by the attorneys if they want a copy	Is aware that a court stenographer will be taking down every word said by every person on the record, but a written transcript may not be available until after the trial is completed

These differences make it important to prepare for trial even though your attorney may have already prepared you for deposition. You received certain guidelines for your deposition that no longer apply at trial, and it is critical that you be aware of these differences. For example, imagine you are at trial and still following the admonition to "be as brief as possible in your answers" when addressing a group of decision-makers who must trust and believe you if they are to decide in favor of your case. Your terseness could easily be interpreted as a failure to be forthcoming, or having something to hide from the jurors, and the negative consequences could be unintended but harmful to your case.

How Questioning Differs

At a deposition, a party or witness is primarily questioned by the opposing party's attorney, and only in rare circumstances will your own attorney question you. There is no benefit to being questioned by your own attorney at a deposition because the telling of your complete story is better saved for trial. Your attorney may not want to show his or her hand by asking you questions that reveal your trial strategy or provide additional evidence not yet discovered by the other side. If your attorney needs to consult with you, this can be done confidentially outside the presence of opposing counsel.

At trial, you will be questioned by your own attorney and by opposing counsel. You are typically called to the stand first by your own attorney. This gives you an opportunity to answer questions and tell your story according to your attorney's plan. You are being questioned under friendly circumstances and the questions will be framed carefully and systematically by your attorney to reveal your testimony in the most convincing and effective light. This is called direct examination.

When your attorney is finished, you are typically cross-examined by the opposing party's attorney. You can expect these questions to be more insinuating and more challenging, and you will likely feel less comfortable answering them. However, it is important that your demeanor under cross-examination remain the same as when you are questioned by your own attorney. You would not want the jurors to assume you have a Jekyll-Hyde personality. Remember that consistency is very important to jurors and to your credibility.

There may also be re-direct, which gives your attorney the opportunity to clear up any answers that were unclear or misleading when you were being cross-examined. Opposing counsel also has an opportunity to re-cross you again. This may go on for several rounds, but extended re-direct and re-cross questioning is relatively rare.

The Importance of Consistency

If you have been deposed, and you are then asked to give testimony at trial, it is very important that your responses are consistent and that you do not change your testimony between deposition and trial. If you should change your testimony, this will be pointed out by opposing counsel, and your testimony will be impeached. This means the attorney can call into question the truthfulness or accuracy of your testimony by showing that your testimony is too inconsistent to be believed. In fact, a judge may instruct jurors that if they believe your testimony is inconsistent, they may disregard all of it! This is why it is very important to read the written transcript of your deposition before you give testimony at trial. That way, you will know what you have said previously so you can be consistent. Your attorney may request that you study carefully certain sections of your deposition transcript because they are particularly important.

If Your Testimony Has Changed

There are circumstances under which your testimony could understand-ably change between deposition and trial. For example, in the intervening time before trial, you may recall something you were unable to remember at the time of your deposition. Meetings with your attorney after your deposition may have refreshed your memory of additional facts or events. Reviewing certain documents or records may show that your memory at the time of the deposition was inaccurate and you now stand corrected. These are legitimate reasons for inconsistencies so it is very important to inform your attorney if you recall additional and/or different information from what you said in your deposition.

Your attorney will have reviewed your deposition before you are called to the stand. He or she will inform you of any anticipated inconsistencies so they can be cleared up in a pre-trial session with your attorney. That way, you will be prepared if any differences in your testimony are chal-lenged in court by opposing counsel.

Credibility Is at Stake

Your credibility is at stake whenever you become involved in a legal case, either as a party, a witness, or a representative of a party. Jurors will be assessing what you say, how you express yourself, what sort of impression you are making on them, and how honest you appear to be. Credibility can be viewed as having three main components.

Elements of Credibility

Confidence

• Do you show certainty and conviction in your answers?

• Are you in control of your testimony?

• Are you speaking with volume, in language that is understandable to all?

• Is it confidence, or is it inflated ego and boasting?

• Do you sit tall and pay attention to the questions?

Likeability

• Are you personable? Do you strike jurors as likeable?

• Do you have an attractive personality or are you hostile, defensive, depressed, or otherwise unapproachable?

• Can you relate to and connect with people?

Honesty

• Can you be believed?

• Are you trustworthy?

• Does your body language and eye contact signal you are telling the truth?

• Are your answers consistent?

When you are on the stand, jurors are not only listening to what you say, but they are evaluating whether you can be believed and trusted. And they tend to make this evaluation early and quickly when you take the stand. Since we tend to believe people that we like, likeability and confidence are important elements that will establish your credibility and the degree of influence your testimony will carry with jurors.

CHAPTER 7

PRE-DEPOSITION AND PRE-TRIAL PREPARATION WITH YOUR ATTORNEY

It is perfectly proper, and highly recommended, to have one or more sessions with your attorney to prepare for giving testimony at a deposition or at trial. Witness-preparation sessions are not held for the purpose of coaching answers or scripting what your attorney believes you should say. Such prompting would be disastrous, and could lead to untruthful answers. Your answers must be your own. It is also not a witness makeover or a secretive attempt to re-construct your testimony so it will be more supportive of the case. Even if that were possible, which it is not, such activity would be unethical. However, an opportunity to ask questions of your attorney, along with some question-answer practice in the expected format, can go a long way toward reducing your anxiety and getting you better prepared to give effective testimony. Remember that the opposing side has spent many months, perhaps years, preparing for trial. They have reviewed documents and planned carefully what they want to ask you. They are ready. You must be also.

Witness Preparation Is Part of the Attorney's Role

If your attorney requests a pre-deposition or pre-trial preparation session, this does not mean your attorney has concerns about your ability to answer questions effectively or considers you to be a poor witness. On the contrary, careful and thorough preparation before you give testimony is part of an attorney's responsibility to ensure that witnesses are well informed and prepared. Your experience as a witness will be much easier, less anxiety-provoking, and more effective if you are well prepared. The goal is to ensure your testimony is more accurate, more believable, and more precise than it might be without careful preparation.

If your attorney has requested that you attend a preparation session, thank him or her and make room on your calendar. If your attorney has not proposed a preparation session, and you realize one is essential for you, take the initiative and request one. Depending on your circumstances, you may even want to insist on one. Remember that not all attorneys conduct such sessions (although we strongly encourage them to do so), and not all sessions may be conducted in the same way, with the same purposes.

Typical Purposes of a Preparation Session

Having a witness-preparation session with your attorney has several important purposes. It will enable you to:

- **Review** areas of testimony your attorney anticipates you will be questioned about. This will help refresh your memory and assist you in thinking through potential responses.

- Get **guidance and suggestions** about how to listen to questions and how to handle difficult questions. This will help reduce your anxiety about potential traps.

- Receive **feedback** about the effectiveness of your responses and how they are likely to be viewed by jurors and others. This will improve your confidence and credibility.

- Get an **explanation** of general procedures and rules. This will help you understand what will happen on the day of your testimony. Any questions you have will also be answered.

- Receive **advice** on your demeanor, dress, and attitude so you will make a good impression.

- **Ease** your anxiety by eliminating some of the unknowns.

People who have had a pre-deposition or pre-trial preparation session (or several, if necessary) agree that it is very helpful. They often remark, "If I had not had the session, I would have been at a great disadvantage. Now I feel like I'm prepared for most anything."

Who Will Attend the Preparation Session

Your attorney(s) will be present for the entire session. Another attorney *may* be present to role-play opposing counsel and make the practice as realistic as possible. Usually this is a colleague who practices in the same specialty area and is familiar with your case.

A communications consultant or litigation psychologist may be there to give you suggestions on how to listen to questions and give your answers most effectively, in your own words. Other attorneys from the firm may be present during the session. If others will be present, your attorney will advise you. You may be prepared as part of a group (such as nurses on a ward, employees from a certain shift) in which there will be both group orientation and individual preparation.

What You Will Do at the Preparation Session

A pre-deposition or pre-trial preparation session is for your benefit, so plan to be actively involved. Your attorney will bring you up to speed on what is happening with your case, answer your questions, and ensure you know the date, time, and location of your appearance.

You will be reviewing areas of questioning that your attorney and you expect. If you are preparing for deposition, the focus will be on cross-examination only. If you are preparing for trial, you will explore both direct (by your attorney) and potential cross-examination questions. Your attorney or a colleague may play the role of opposing counsel and pose questions to you as he or she might. There may be several hours of such Q&A. The attorney and others on your legal team may provide feedback on how to improve the effectiveness of your listening and the effectiveness of your responses.

You will be encouraged *not* to memorize answers. The goal is to help you feel more comfortable with the Q&A process, since this is a foreign way of communicating in the non-attorney world. You may also review key documents (such as reports, scene photos, administrative policies, medical records) and the timeline relevant to your case in order to refresh your memory.

Your attorney cannot know all the questions you are likely to be asked in a deposition or at trial, but based on past experience, he or she will know many of them. Your attorney may be able to share insights into opposing counsel's style and demeanor. However, just as people differ in their communication patterns, attorneys differ in their questioning style, and you should be prepared for the unexpected.

How You Should Prepare for the Session

To get maximum benefit from a preparation session, both you and the attorney must get ready for it. The attorney will prepare by drafting sample questions of various types (open-ended, hypothetical, compound, etc.), and you must also be ready. A day or two before your session, you should complete as many of the following as possible:

- Review all relevant documents, as instructed by your attorney. Valuable time will be wasted if you do not know your records and documents beforehand.

- Refresh your memory about relevant events, parties, and dates.

- Write out three questions about which you are most concerned, most anxious, or most uncertain about how to answer.

- Dress as you plan to dress for deposition or trial so your attorney can assess the appropriateness of your clothing. Remember that you want to make a good impression on opposing counsel so s/he can assess your jury appeal. If you are going to trial, you want to make certain your clothing is appropriate for the courtroom.

- Think about the questions you want to ask the attorney about the case or the trial process so they can be answered during the session.

- Get a good night's rest.

While your attorney may ask you to bring certain documents with you to the preparation session, you should never bring anything with you to the actual deposition or to trial unless your attorney has specifically directed you to do so. Anything in your possession can be reviewed by opposing counsel.

What to Ask Your Attorney at a Preparation Session

If you are unfamiliar with the deposition or trial process, ask your attorney to explain the general procedures and rules that will be followed. This will help reduce the unknowns and give you a better understanding of what to expect. You may ask your attorney to explain who will be in attendance at the deposition or in court, who will be asking questions (and who will not), and about how long the deposition or your trial testimony is expected to last.

A written transcript is made of exactly what each person said in the deposition, and you have a right to a copy of it. It is wise to keep your copy until the lawsuit is concluded. Your attorney will also have a copy. If you are asked to give testimony later at trial, you will want to re-read your deposition transcript to make certain your testimony at trial is consistent with your deposition answers. Ask your attorney to supply you with a copy of your deposition if you are expected to give testimony at trial.

Your deposition may also be recorded on video. Ask your attorney if the deposition will be videotaped, as this may affect how you dress. You may also want to know about the swearing-in process, the roles of the court stenographer and videographer (if one is to be present), and the way in which objections will be handled. If you are preparing to give trial testimony, make certain to ask the attorney for a brief description of the steps of a trial and where your testimony fits in. And don't forget to make certain you know the location, date, and time of the preparation session.

How Long the Preparation Session Will Last

Although most witness-preparation sessions last between two and five hours, there is considerable variability in their length. The extent of your preparation session will depend on several factors:

- Your role in the case and how extensive your testimony is expected to be.

- The initial assessment of your communication patterns and whether those patterns will require some adjustment to make certain you are listening and responding carefully.

- How thoroughly you have already refreshed your memory about events and any documents involved in the case.

- Your level of cooperation and your ability to incorporate feedback about how to improve your listening or speaking skills.

- Your past experience in giving a deposition or trial testimony.

- The amount of time you and your attorney have available for the session.

If you are particularly anxious, if your involvement in the case is complex and spans a long time period, or if you are having difficulty adjusting to the question-answer format of a deposition or trial testimony, your attorney may suggest another preparation session at a later date. Make yourself available for any recommended follow-up sessions. Remember that your attorney is experienced in knowing how judges and jurors respond to witness testimony and the attorney's advice about your effectiveness should be sought out.

What to Do if You Are Asked about Preparation Sessions

Pre-deposition or pre-trial preparation sessions with your attorney are considered "attorney-client protected." This means you cannot be asked about them because communications between you and your attorney, whether written or oral, are confidential. If you are asked a question by opposing counsel that requires you to reveal information shared between you and your attorney, your attorney will object and instruct you not to answer. Follow her or his instruction.

If you are being deposed, you may also be asked: "What have you done to prepare for your deposition?" Without revealing the content of any communications you have had with your attorney (remember, this is privileged), you may simply say: "I have met with my attorney and reviewed records pertinent to my involvement in this case." You are not required to answer questions about what you have done to prepare for your *case*, as this is privileged. For example, if your attorney has directed you to research documents, prepare a timeline, or read certain materials he or she has prepared, this is privileged and you cannot be asked about it.

CHAPTER 8

THE NEED TO
LISTEN DIFFERENTLY

Most of what we learn, we learn by listening. Yet most of us aren't good listeners. In their book, *Excellence in Business Communication*, the authors write, "Listening is a far more complex process than most people think…most of us listen at or below a 25 percent efficiency rate, remember only about half of what's said during a 10-minute conversation, and forget half of that within 48 hours." For those who consider themselves good listeners, this is sobering information. In addition, most people are unaware of how inaccurate their listening truly is, even in important situations, such as when a doctor is giving a patient medication information or follow-up care instructions.

It shouldn't be surprising that many people are poor listeners. First of all, most of us have not been taught how to listen. We learn how to read, write, and speak, but not how to listen. Secondly, if we make listening (or speaking) errors, we can usually correct them later, without significant consequences. Lastly, we juggle so many activities at work and at home that we don't give much thought to listening. In our current world of information overload, speaking tends to take priority over listening. Unfortunately, people are fired, customers are lost, and relationships are strained because of ineffective listening.

In the legal arena, the consequences of poor listening are quite serious. In fact, the number one mistake made by all witnesses—fact witnesses, expert witnesses, supportive family members, personal representatives—is the failure to listen carefully to what is being asked. This is because we are accustomed to social listening—listening with the intent of understanding the underlying meaning, discerning relevant emotions, and thinking ahead about how to respond in an appropriate and effective manner. When giving a deposition or testifying at trial, common errors that are forgiven or overlooked in social situations can result in a nonresponsive answer, an inaccurate response, or a misleading statement, none of which may be intended.

Listening Errors

When it comes to listening errors, two types are very common:

a) **Out-listening:** This is what happens when we listen to a speaker only long enough to determine what she is probably going to say, and then we tune out until we hear another word or phrase that recaptures our attention. In between, our minds wander, or we start thinking about what we will say in reply. Out-listening becomes a habit in a world of information-overload, and it can be problematic when you are testifying. The biggest problem is that out-listening leaves you not with a memory of what the speaker actually said, but of what you *think* was said. If your mind has wandered or you do not understand the question, ask for clarification in simple terms: "I didn't understand your question. Could you repeat it?"

b) **Selective listening:** This is when we hear only what we *want* to hear and filter out the remainder. Our way of looking at a subject also shapes how much of a message we receive and retain. It is our mental filter through which information is screened before it is actually comprehended—our particular spin on things. A dozen people may hear the same message—and give a dozen different versions of what was said. Remember the childhood game of "Pass It On" or "Telephone"? Responding to what you *think* you heard can lead to very inaccurate interpretations.

The only way to avoid these listening errors is to be aware of them and to practice listening to what is being said or asked before you allow yourself to think about your answer. Most attorneys agree that the best witnesses are the best listeners. Practice listening at home and work by repeating what you heard: "I heard you say [statement]. Is that correct?" You will be surprised at the feedback you receive about the inaccuracy of what you think you heard!

Techniques for Improving Your Listening Skill

Several methods have been shown to be helpful in improving your attentiveness when being questioned at a deposition or at trial. If you find yourself out-listening or listening selectively (as described above), try the following techniques.

Ways to Improve Listening Accuracy

• Imagine the question being typed out in front of your eyes as you hear it. READ the question rather than listening to it.

• Mentally repeat the question EXACTLY as it was asked, without any filtering or distortion. You will be surprised at how difficult this is, but it gets easier with practice.

• Avoid evaluating the question or judging its relevance, and focus exclusively on the WORDS being used.

• FOCUS your attention and ignore other distractions such as outside noise. Remind yourself how important listening is in the legal arena where words carry great weight.

• Watch out for emotional TRIGGERS that may cause you to tune out. Certain words can arouse strong emotions and cause us to stop listening to anything further.

• Force yourself to WAIT until the question is asked completely before you begin thinking about your response. Don't interrupt the questioner.

• REPEAT what you heard: "Let me make sure I heard correctly. You are asking me if…Is that correct?"

• INCLUDE part of the question in your answer. This will force you to listen to the exact words used by the attorney.

One of the best ways to improve your listening skill is to practice. Practice listening carefully to one person for an entire day (this can be tiring!). Practice listening by mentally typing out everything said during a conversation sometime with a coworker or family member. Practice repeating back what you heard someone say. Nudge yourself to listen better for an entire day.

Don't Overdo It

In practicing your listening skills, don't get carried away. Avoid nodding your head or repeatedly saying "yes" during a question to indicate you are listening and that you understand what the questioner is asking. This can get you in trouble if your eventual answer is "no." Although eye contact can signal you are paying attention, it is not necessary to stare at the questioner at all times. It is also not necessary to incline your head toward the questioner, or tilt your head as though giving the person your ear. All things in moderation.

CHAPTER 9

TAKING CONTROL
OF YOUR ANSWERS

What worries witnesses the most? The greatest worry, and the greatest fear, is that a skilled attorney will ask probing questions that will force you to say something unintended, and you will sabotage the case. Fear of being intimidated, manipulated, and bullied dominate the worry list of many witnesses, regardless of their level of education, profession, or experience with the legal system. However, just as in any other contest, knowing the rules, understanding the process, and taking control of your verbal volleys will help to level out the playing field. Let's start with the process.

Best Way to Answer Any Question

Although your attorney will know the areas in which you can be expected to be questioned, there is no way for him or her to know exactly what you will be asked, how questions will be phrased, or the order in which they will be put to you. The best way to address any question, regardless of its content is to follow five basic steps, without fail. These steps are listed in the following table. Chapter 10 provides suggestions for how to best answer various *kinds* of questions.

Five Steps for Answering Questions

1. LISTEN very carefully to the question. Hear every word. Avoid listening just long enough to get the gist because you may not hear it accurately. Repeat the question mentally exactly as it was asked, without any filtering or second-guessing. Practice what was learned in the chapter on listening.

2. PAUSE to make certain the attorney has finished the question and to allow time for any objections to be made.

3. THINK about exactly what you want to say. Take your time. Keep the pace slow. Think before you speak.

4. ANSWER the question asked, and only the question asked. Be succinct and don't ramble. Don't answer off the top of your head. Consider every answer important, even the short ones.

5. STOP TALKING. Some attorneys use silence as a technique to keep you talking. Just end your answer and wait for the next question.

This all sounds basic and easy, right? Not so. The question-and-answer format of a deposition (and of trial testimony) is not only unfamiliar, it is very challenging. Remember that every word you speak is being recorded, and in that respect it is set in stone. So think carefully before you speak and avoid simply saying whatever comes to mind. Make certain the words you use are your own; don't simply agree with what the attorney says. While "yes," "no," and "I don't know" are the easiest and the quickest answers, rarely are they complete and truthful answers. Use your own words to say precisely what you want to say.

You Are in Control

Most people assume that in a deposition or at trial, the attorneys are in control because they know the law, the rules, and how to handle witnesses. Nothing could be further from the truth. The witness always has the most control. In fact, you are in control of nearly every aspect of your testimony. What exactly do you control?

You control the **pace.** An attorney cannot ask another question until you have completed your answer to the previous one, so you can take the time you need to think before you speak. By taking time to think about what you want to say, taking a breath of air, and then giving your answer, you set the pace of questioning. The pace of questioning you set should not be a tennis (rapid volley) pace, but more like a golf (slow and deliberate) pace. Take your time. Be comfortable with pauses and silences. Remember that once you have answered the question, you should stop talking. Avoid the need to fill silences by continuing to talk. Also, never interrupt the question to begin your answer. Wait until the attorney has completed the question, pause, and then answer. Trying to answer quickly will not speed up the process; it will only make you appear rude and impulsive.

You control the **clarity** of questions. It is important to let the attorney know, through your demeanor and communication, that you are there to cooperate and answer questions. However, you must be firm in insisting that if the attorney wants a clear, simple, and fair answer, he or she must reciprocate by asking clear and reasonable questions that you are qualified to answer. Remember that you should never speculate, guess, estimate, or stall if you are uncertain about your answer or do not have a clear and honest answer. If your first impulse is to simply say something/anything in order to move things along, you will undoubtedly regret it later.

You control the **content** of your answers. Despite what most witnesses fear, it is impossible for attorneys to put words in your mouth, twist what you say, or make you sound stupid or incompetent unless you allow them to do so. If you listen very carefully to the questions, and give very specific answers to those questions, it is nearly impossible for an attorney to testify for you by twisting what you say. No one—not the judge, not the attorneys, not the jurors—saw the events as you saw them, performed the activity as you did, or applied your knowledge as you thought appropriate, so don't allow anyone to testify for you.

You control the **completeness** of your answer. A skillful attorney may try to cut off your answer or quickly interject another. But an incomplete answer could be misleading. Always complete your answer. If you are interrupted, say politely, "I'm sorry, but you interrupted my answer before I was finished. Please let me finish and then I will answer your next question."

You control the **accuracy** of your answer. If you discover during your testimony at deposition or trial that you have given an inaccurate or incorrect answer to a previous question, you should correct it as soon as possible. Say politely, "I'm sorry, I misunderstood a previous question. When you asked me about [issue], my answer should have been [correct answer]." Or you might say, "I realize now that I may have misspoken in a previous answer. When you asked me about [issue], I meant to say that [correct answer]."

You control the **precision** of your answer. Your answer should be as precise as the question or context requires. Consider the following exchange:

> Q: *Mr. Smith, have you ever seen a rental contract exactly like this one?*
>
> A: *No.*

Everyone knows that nearly every contract is slightly different. Therefore, the answer should be "no." But with that answer, jurors could conclude the witness was not qualified to evaluate the contract, or that there was something fishy about this one. Therefore, a more precise answer might be the following:

> A: *In my years of experience, I have seen hundreds of rental contracts, but I can't say that any of them were exactly like this one because contracts are rarely exactly alike.*

A skillful attorney may also misquote your prior testimony, either intentionally or unintentionally. You should immediately correct this so your answer remains precise. Sometimes misquotes are subtle, but remember that the point is to be precise. For example, if you said "between fifty to sixty miles an hour" and the attorney summarizes it as "sixty miles per hour," you should correct this by saying, "I said earlier that I was driving fifty to sixty miles an hour, not sixty."

Although you may feel that lawyers have superior knowledge (and perhaps more education) than you, they actually have less control in the questioning process than you. It might surprise you to learn that many attorneys are just as nervous about questioning you as you are about being questioned. Their fear is that you will say something unexpected that hurts their case or promotes yours. A common saying among trial attorneys is "Never ask a witness a question at trial to which you do not already know the answer." Your fear of what questions may be asked is balanced by their fear of what you might say in response.

Focus Your Answers

Keep your answers concise, on point with what was asked, and truthful. Never, never, never exaggerate, distort, or misrepresent facts. You will almost always be caught and your entire testimony will be called into question. This is called "impeaching" a witness and it can have serious consequences. Better to admit an unfortunate fact than to misrepresent it.

Avoid wandering and giving background or history when answering questions unless specifically asked to do so. Nothing is more aggravating for jurors than to listen to a witness blah-blah-blah about something that is not directly relevant to the question being asked. Control your desire to entertain or enlighten jurors with interesting stories or favored quotes from Shakespeare or the Bible. Stick to the question at hand. Consider the following excerpt from a deposition:

> Q: *Did your wife accompany you so she could drive you home after the medical procedure?*
>
> A: *Yes, she did. And it was a scary ride because she doesn't like to drive on the freeway and she gets very nervous when she has to. She never took a driver's ed class so she pretty much drives only around the neighborhood. I just never had the time to really teach her.*

The witness should have stopped the answer after "Yes, she did." All that came after that was nonresponsive and unnecessary.

If you know that your answer will be long, complicated, or technical, warn people by first saying, for example, "My answer will be a bit complex, and I'll do my best to simplify it." This preface lets others know to be prepared for a longer answer than they may expect.

Avoid Absolutes and Exactness

Using absolute words such as "always," "never," "in every case," and "completely" can lock in your testimony, so you should avoid them. Use qualifiers such as "about," "normally," "usually," "typically," "not all the time," "generally," "it depends," "most of the time," and "approximately." You avoid traps this way. Also, absolutes tend to be hard for others to believe. A witness who says she has "never" driven over the speed limit is likely to be doubted and viewed as untruthful. Is such a statement really worth having your credibility challenged? Use qualifiers any time you feel an attorney is trying to lock in your testimony. Here are several examples:

> Q: *You've told us about all the medical problems you have had since the accident. Does that cover everything?*
>
> A: *That is all I can think of at this time.*
>
> Q: *Do you read the package inserts that accompany medications that you pick up at the pharmacy?*
>
> A: *I usually do.*
>
> Q: *Your policy manual states that you must inform second tier managers of a change in compensation within two days of a decision. Have you ever deviated from that policy?*
>
> A: *We typically follow the policy.*

Note how the qualified answer leaves room for additional testimony you may recall later.

Avoid exactness in answers unless you are certain about the accuracy of your answer. This is especially true when speaking about dates, times of day, amounts, distances, details of conversation, location features, and other details.

When Memory Fails You

Many people are concerned that their memory will fail them, particularly when faced with an important question about events that may have occurred months or even years earlier. When memories fail, most people believe their case is weakened by answers such as "I don't know" or "I don't remember." You may feel pressured to give an answer because you don't want to appear stupid or evasive. In reality, everyone's memory fails or becomes incomplete at some point. This is to be expected and no apologies are needed. It is unacceptable, however, to fake memory loss or lack of knowledge simply to avoid answering a difficult question.

Jurors and judges can be frustrated and unsatisfied when a witness answers a question with "I don't know" or "I don't recall," even when that is the honest answer. Under these circumstances, it can be helpful, and more effective, to explain *why* you don't know or don't recall. For example:

> "I don't recall where we went after leaving the office. It was several years ago."

> "I don't know why the evaluation was not placed in the file. I was not her supervisor at the time."

> "I can't recall the details and I don't want to make assumptions or guess."

Such answers are more satisfying and explanatory than a verbal shrug, and will lend credibility to your testimony. Jurors understand that not every question will be followed by a complete answer, but they do expect a response that makes sense to them.

In some cases, you may not have a clear memory of an event or an action you took, but you can be certain it happened in a specific way because of your customs, habits, and practices. For example, you may not recall the name of every street at which you stopped for a red light, but you know you stopped at every red light you encountered on the way to work because it is your habit and practice to do so. You know that your seat belt was on because it is your habit to lock it in place before you start your engine. You know that you locked the door when you left your store on Wednesday night because that is the last item on your mental close-up list. The point is that you can answer a question based on your practices and habits even if you do not have a clear and detailed memory of it.

Never Guess or Speculate

Perhaps the three most challenging words of admission are: "I don't know." We fear that admitting we lack knowledge will signal our incompetence, poor memory, or lack of intelligence. But if your response to a question begins with a qualifier such as "I'm not sure, but..." or "My guess would be that..." then your answer should instead be "I don't know." Guessing or speculation tends to be heard by attorneys and jurors as near certainty. This could lock you into a difficult situation. If you are not certain, do not speculate, guess, estimate, or assume; just say, "I'm not certain" or "I don't know." Or, you might qualify your answer, such as in the following examples:

> Q: *What time did time you arrive back at your home?*
>
> A: *I'm not certain of the exact time, but I recall it was between 8:00 PM and 9:00 PM.*
>
> Q. *Do you have a recollection of that conversation?*
>
> A. *I remember that the conversation happened, but three years later I cannot remember exactly what was said.*

If you do not remember something clearly, do not hesitate to say so.

Failures in memory are expected because we all have the experience of forgetting. Remember, however, that answering with "I don't know" or "I don't recall" as a means of avoiding a truthful response that may be embarrassing or incriminating is always a bad idea. Jurors will see through it easily and wonder what you are hiding.

Watch for Inflammatory or Ambiguous Words

Some attorneys have an inclination to use inflammatory, emotion-laden, or ambiguous terms that are embedded in the questions they ask or the way in which they summarize events or circumstances. Examples might be words such as *profound, extreme, traumatic, severe, agonizing, dangerous, stressful, exceptional, significant, extraordinary, misleading, devastating, incomplete, numerous, botched, mistake, hurtful, harmful, tragic, frightening,* and so on. Such words can mean vastly different things to different people. What we might consider "excessive" bleeding might be "minimal" to a surgeon. What a mother considers "wildly dangerous," a young single person might describe as "exciting." Our own experiences play a large role in the language we use to describe them.

Be careful about the use of descriptive terms when being questioned by an attorney. Before you agree that an event was stressful, for example, make certain there is a joint understanding of the meaning of the term. If you doubt such agreement, ask for clarification, or specify your meaning as part of your answer. Here are several examples of how you could respond:

> Q: *Did you witness Joe receiving the traumatic blow to his midsection during the tackle?*
>
> A: *I'm not certain what you mean by traumatic. Can you clarify what you mean? OR*
>
> A: *I saw him being tackled from behind and thrown to the ground. That is fairly common in football.*

Q: *How many times did Ms. Jones complain about the hostility she was getting from co-workers on a frequent basis?*

A: *She told me on two occasions that several coworkers had made hurtful remarks about her husband being on disability.*

Note that in these examples the witness avoided using the attorney's words. Instead, the witness answered more accurately by using his own words.

When the Opposing Attorney Is Annoying

Some attorneys, like some people, are simply annoying. Whether they are naturally annoying, or simply acting in a certain fashion in order to generate an emotional response on your part, annoying attorneys present a special challenge. Typical annoying behaviors to be on the lookout for include:

Responding to your answer in a condescending manner, such as:

- "That wasn't my question."
- "You obviously weren't listening to my question."
- "I heard your answer, but now I want an honest answer."
- "Do you really expect jurors to believe that response?"

This way of reacting to your answer is designed to imply you are a poor listener, stupid, or not believable. It usually works, and the witness feels bad and tries even harder to please the attorney, often by changing his or her answer. Don't fall for this.

Asking questions in a provocative or sarcastic manner, such as:

- "You were too busy texting to be looking where you were going, weren't you?"
- "Extra classes were offered, but you didn't think you needed to take them, did you?"

- "That's not the whole truth now, is it?"

- "You thought you were so indispensable to the company that you could never be fired, didn't you?"

An equally snide or nasty response will have little or no effect on the attorney. But it will show others in the deposition or the courtroom that you are capable of being snide and nasty. It is doubtful that this will help, and will likely harm your case, so avoid it. Simply answer the question as if it were asked in a normal tone of voice.

Asking absurdly detailed questions, such as:

- "What grades did you get in each of the classes you took in your firefighting training?"

- "How many times have you driven down Nelson Road after dark?"

- "Where were you on the evening of July 14, 1998?"

While it may be easy to respond to such questions in a tone of voice that reflects your own annoyance with the attorney's demeanor, resist the urge. Aim for an even keel in your emotional status, regardless of how annoying, accusatory, or snide the attorney becomes. That is how you show your patience and stamina.

Not all attorneys are organized, nor do they necessarily ask questions in a logical sequence. Do not become distracted if the attorney's questions jump around. This could reflect a specific strategy on his or her part to throw you off, or it could simply reflect a lack of preparation or organization on the attorney's part. Just remain focused on the question in front of you.

Concerns about Your Speech

If you speak with an accent, speak very slowly. It takes people longer to process English (or any language) if it is spoken with an accent. Make a special effort to articulate your words carefully, even if it means exaggerating the slowness with which you speak. Your efforts will be appreciated by the attorneys, the stenographer who must take down every word spoken, and the jurors who need to understand what you are saying.

If you have a speech impediment such as a lisp, stutter, or stammer, let your attorney know if it worsens or becomes more noticeable when you are nervous. S/he can then alert opposing counsel, the court stenographer, and the jurors so you won't feel embarrassed.

CHAPTER 10

KINDS OF QUESTIONS TO EXPECT

As a witness, you may be asked many kinds of questions, in different contexts, with varying forms of expression, in a wide variety of styles, by attorneys with different communication patterns. This chapter will help you become more familiar with the nature of questions, how they may be posed to you, and how you can best respond to difficult questions.

Kinds of Questions Often Asked

There are many different kinds of questions, but the types most likely to be asked at a deposition or at trial are summarized below, along with an example of each.

Type of Question	Example
Open-ended or very general: Designed to elicit a general response or simply to get you talking.	"What can you tell me about your educational background?"
Closed-end: Designed to limit your answer to a simple yes or no response.	"Isn't it true that you did not sign the contract until two weeks after work began?"
Hypothetical: Theoretical, based on a supposition or assumption; asks the witness to "imagine" a specific scenario.	"Let's assume the road was slightly wet from an earlier rain. What would have been the appropriate speed to be driving on that road?"

Compound: Two or more questions posed at once.	"When did you leave Dr. Smith's care and why did you switch doctors?"
Unclear: Uses a term that is not understood or whose meaning can vary; fails to define the context.	"Have you ever been fired for disciplinary reasons?" (Unclear what is meant by disciplinary reasons.)
Confusing: Question is convoluted or difficult to follow.	"Were you concerned with the level of steroid that was being injected that you can't start or stop quickly or you thought it wouldn't have a systemic effect?"
Embedded assumption: Implanted in the question is an erroneous or inaccurate assumption.	"When did you stop beating your spouse?"
Leading: Suggests the answer, usually in the hope you will simply agree.	"When Jim told you he was having dark thoughts, you assumed he was thinking about suicide, right?"
Misleading assumption: Includes an assumption about your actions that misrepresents what actually happened.	"So after you took off speeding down the road, you realized you had left the car seat at the house, right?"
Overly simplified: A general question that may sound accurate, but lacks important specificity.	"Wouldn't you agree that if you live in America, you should love America?"

By now you are asking yourself how you can possibly remember all these different kinds of questions, or differentiate between them. It's easier than it appears. You hear these kinds of questions every day, from "Do you want plastic or paper?" at the grocery store, to "Who were you on the phone with and what did they say?" You probably have simply never thought to classify the type of question you were being asked. You will not be required to do so at a deposition or when giving trial testimony, but knowing the underlying form of a question will enable you to answer it more effectively than if you treat every question the same way.

Responding to Different Kinds of Questions

What should you do when asked a compound question, or a question containing an erroneous assumption? Here are some examples of ways to respond to questions that appear confusing, limiting, misleading, or in any way difficult to answer.

Open-ended or overly general:

Example: *"How would you describe your early years growing up in Detroit?"*

Suggestion #1—Ask for more specificity: *"I'm not sure what period of my youth you are referring to. Can you give me a timeframe?"*

Suggestion #2—Give an equally general answer: *"It was fairly typical—family, school, friends, church."*

Closed-end:

Example: *"Isn't it true that you knew the oil leases were fraudulent months before they were issued? Just answer me yes or no."*

Suggestion #1—Refuse to answer with a simple word: *"I can't give a complete answer if I'm confined to a simple yes or no."*

Suggestion #2—Qualify the answer without quibbling: *"I knew there were concerns about the leases, but I did not know they were fraudulent."*

Suggestion #3—Answer briefly but hint there is a longer explanation: *"No, I did not know they were fraudulent and I will be glad to explain why."*

Hypothetical:

Example: *"Assume there is no set procedure regarding how the lift was to be operated. What is the greatest safety concern the operator should be aware of?"*

Suggestion #1—Refuse to make the assumption: "*I cannot imagine that scenario, so I can't answer that question.*"

Suggestion #2—Make certain your answer is hypothetical: "*In that hypothetical scenario, my hypothetical answer would be that personal safety comes first.*"

Suggestion #3—Stretch the odds: "*I imagine anything is possible, including your hypothetical scenario, but it would be highly unlikely.*"

Compound:

Example: "What time did you leave your workplace and who was still on shift when you left?"

Suggestion #1—Ask for one question at a time: "*You have given two questions. Which one do you want me to answer first?*"

Suggestion #2—Separate the questions and answer each in turn: "*You have asked me two questions. My answer to the first is that I left work at 6:15 PM, and my answer to the second is that Carol and Terry were still there when I left.*"

Unclear:

Example: "What incidental factors were at play the day you drove the bus to Hartford?"

Suggestion #1—Ask for clarification: "*I don't understand what you mean by 'incidental factors.' Can you be more specific?*"

Suggestion #2—Clarify it yourself: "*If you mean by 'incidental factors' the weather reports and snowfall levels for that day, let me review those and I can answer your question.*"

Anytime a noun or adjective is used that could have different meanings to different people (for example: alarming, traumatic, serious, prejudicial, stressful, etc.), don't assume you and the questioner define it the same way. If you have any doubt, ask for clarification or a definition.

Confusing:

If you do not understand a question exactly as it was asked, simply say, "I don't understand your question." or "I'm not following that question. Can you ask it differently?" You should never answer a question you do not fully understand. In fact, a common preface made by many attorneys at the beginning of a deposition is to ask, "If you answer my question, is it fair for me to assume you both heard and understood my question?" If you answer a question you did not fully understand, you cannot later claim a misunderstanding. If you are not perfectly clear about what is being asked, say so.

You should not mentally improve a poor question and answer your improved version.

> **Example:** *"How many times did you punch into work late in January of 2009?"*
>
>> A: *"I think you mean more than five minutes after start time, which is considered 'late,' so I'll say four times."*

Also, do not admit you do not understand the question, and then proceed to answer it anyway. For example:

> **Example:** *"What are the various routes you take in making your deliveries?"*
>
>> A: *"I'm not sure what you mean by 'deliveries,' but I would say that I have a main route and then depending upon traffic, I may take one of several alternative routes because I have to make a certain number of deliveries every day and sometimes traffic gets me behind."*

Both of the answers given above could get the witness in trouble. By assuming a definition in the first example, the witness has actually helped opposing counsel, something you should avoid. In the second example, the witness rambled out of uncertainty and may have even suggested he speeds occasionally.

If you get a question you think is confusing, here are some responses that may be helpful:

> Suggestion #1—Ask for clarification: *"I didn't follow you on that question. Could you ask it differently?"*

> Suggestion #2—Refuse to answer: *"I can't answer that question the way you asked it because it made no sense to me."*

Embedded assumption:

We have all heard reference to the question, "So, when did you stop beating your spouse?"—a classic example of a question containing an embedded assumption. Surprisingly, many people answer such questions without challenging the assumption because they are not listening for it and are not expecting it. Watch out! If you ignore the embedded assumption or mis-characterization, an affirmative answer suggests you agree with it. As part of your answer, you must either address the embedded assumption, or disagree with it. Here are some examples of ways to answer a question with an embedded assumption:

Example: *"How fast were you speeding when you hit the patch of ice?"*

> Suggestion #1—*"I can't agree that I was speeding before I hit the patch of ice. Would you still like me to answer the question?"*

> Suggestion #2—*"Your question implies I was speeding, and I was driving the speed limit when I hit the patch of ice."*

> Suggestion #3—*"Your question implies I was speeding, and I was not."*

Example: *"Other than the student center work, how many other painting jobs have you botched?"*

> Suggestion #1—*"I didn't botch the student center painting job. It merely took a little longer than I expected."*

Suggestion #2—*"You're implying the student center painting job was botched, and it was not."*

The important point to remember is that if you fail to catch the embedded assumption and then either deny or correct it, you run the risk of misrepresenting your testimony. This is yet another good reason to listen very carefully to the entire question and the specific words and phrases it contains.

Leading:

Example: **"When you entered the park, you intended to meet with other members of the gang, isn't that correct?"**

Suggestion #1—Resist the tendency to simply agree: *"I didn't know if other members of the group would be there or not."*

Suggestion #2—Reply in your own words: *"My purpose for heading into the park was that it was a shortcut to my uncle's house. That's when I ran into the guys."*

Misleading assumption:

Example: **"So after you were told about the side effects of the drug you had been prescribed, how many pills did you actually take over the course of the next week?"**

Suggestion #1—Correct the misleading assumption: *"First of all, I was never told about any side effects. I was just told to take two pills every day, which I did."*

Suggestion #2—Point out the misleading part of the question: *"You are assuming I was told about the side effects, and I was not."*

Overly simplified:

Example: **"Children should love and respect their parents, shouldn't they?"**

Suggestion #1—Qualify your answer: *"In general this is true, but it depends on the situation and the parent-child relationship. Not all children are able to love and respect their parents."*

Suggestion #2—Disagree and explain: *"I disagree with that generalization. Sometimes it is not possible for a child to love and respect the parents, especially when parents are very abusive."*

These are some examples of the kinds of questions you may be asked that are difficult to answer. There may be others, such as questions that attempt to put words in your mouth, questions that ask for speculation, and questions that emphasize minor details or inconsistencies. The point is that unless you are listening carefully for common traps, it will be easy to give an answer that is misleading or inaccurate. It is up to you to avoid being trapped by making sure you always speak in your own words and do not simply agree with the attorney's words.

The Context of Questions

In real estate it is said that the three most important factors are "location, location, location." In answering questions, the three most important elements are "context, context, context." By context we mean the framework, situation, or perspective related to the question. To avoid misunderstanding, or giving an inaccurate answer, it is important to understand the context of the question. These are the four main contexts of concern to you as a witness:

Contexts to Consider

IN GENERAL vs. IN THIS INSTANCE

PAST vs. PRESENT

BEFORE vs. AFTER

HYPOTHETICAL vs. ACTUAL

When answering questions, it is important for you to be clear about whether the issue relates to something in general, or a specific event or action. Overly general questions leave you wondering where to begin. For example, if someone asked you to tell them about the Earth, or how you learned to be an effective teacher, or what your childhood was like growing up, you would struggle with how to give a succinct answer to such a broad question. Consider these examples of very general questions:

Q: *Tell me about the treatment you provided to Mrs. Smith.*

Q: *What is your background and work history?*

Q: *How did your relationship with the Jones family begin?*

Q: *What are your company's practices with regard to safety?*

Q: *What is the best way to approach an intersection?*

Often, an attorney asks a very broad or general question in a fishing expedition to simply learn how you will handle it and how much information can be gotten from you. This is often an effective technique, and witnesses may go on endlessly, offering information that was not sought.

There are several ways to deal effectively with **overly-broad** or **general** questions:

1. Ask for more specificity: "What is it about my background you wish to know?" or "What specific information are you seeking?" or "That is a very general question; can you narrow it down a bit?" or "Do you mean intersections in general, or the one at Fourth and Adam Streets where the accident occurred?"

2. Give an equally general or broad answer: "We have safety practices in place in many areas of the company," or "I have a degree in drafting and have worked at various companies as a drafter for the past ten years," or "I treated Mrs. Smith with analgesics and light massage."

When answering questions, it is also important to be clear about whether the inquiry relates to some **past condition/event**, or **what is now known**. For example:

> Q: *What did you know about your mother's medical condition?*

Does the questioner mean before or after she was seen in the emergency room? If you are uncertain, seek clarification of context by asking, "What point in time are you referring to?"

Some questions may be unclear about whether the context refers to situations **before the event** at issue, **or after.** For example:

> Q: *What were the sales people told about providing loaner cars to customers whose vehicles were in the garage for repair?*

Does the questioner mean before the customer was involved in an accident with a loaner car, or immediately after the sales staff heard about the accident? If you are uncertain about the context, it is appropriate to request clarification by asking, "Do you mean before the accident or afterward?"

Lastly, when answering questions, be certain you understand whether the question is referring to a **hypothetical** context, or an **actual** one. Hypothetical questions often begin like these examples:

> *"If…"*
>
> *"Let's assume that…"*
>
> *"For purposes of discussion,"*
>
> *"Let's imagine that…"*
>
> *"Let's suppose that…"*
>
> *"Wouldn't it be reasonable to…"*

Such questions pose an imagined scenario and ask you to respond as if the scenario were real. These are difficult questions to answer because most hypotheticals are incomplete; it is impossible to include all the relevant facts. The best way to respond to a hypothetical question is with a qualified answer, such as, "In this hypothetical scenario, my best guess would be that..." You might find yourself unable to picture the hypothetical scenario and you should say so. Here are two examples of how a hypothetical question was handled well:

> Q. *Wouldn't you agree with me that it would be feasible to add a safety device that would sound an alarm if the equipment was about to tip over?*
>
> A: *It would be feasible, but not necessary or practical.*
>
> Q: *Let's assume the safety valve was defective on the day that John was monitoring the steam level. What would be the consequences when the steam level reached 350?*
>
> A: *That is a scenario I can't imagine, so I cannot answer your question.*

Don't Suggest a Better Question

Avoid suggesting a better question than you were asked. It is not your responsibility to make certain a question is clear. Here is an example of a witness who was trying to be helpful, but who inadvertently provided a better question than opposing counsel had formulated, much to her own attorney's annoyance.

> Q: *What was supposed to be included in the contract?*
>
> A: *I think what you really want to know is what elements I am required to include in any leasing contract involving a term of less than two years. My answer is...*

The best response is a simple one: "Can you be more specific?" Although it is tempting to help opposing counsel, or to help move a slow deposition along, you should never do opposing counsel's job for him or her.

Don't Anticipate Questions

Avoid playing lawyer by trying to figure out why an attorney is asking you a certain question or what s/he is likely to ask next. This will distract you from listening to the question and composing a truthful and precise answer. The attorney may have no particular path or reason for the questions; they could simply be part of the attorney's standard set of questions. Don't assume the line of questioning is relevant to anything other than for the attorney to examine the limits of your knowledge or experience with the events at issue.

Avoid trying to anticipate where the line of questioning is headed. One of the authors once viewed the video-recorded deposition of a hotel executive who had paused several minutes between questions. The attorney was concerned about how this might be perceived if the witness acted similarly in a jury trial. When asked in a pre-trial preparation session the reason for the long pauses, he responded, "I'm thinking through various scenarios in my head so I can prepare for all the different avenues the attorney might go down." In trying to out-maneuver the attorney, the executive came across as uninformed, belligerent, and "taking time to make up answers"—not at all what he intended. The lesson to be learned is that there is simply no way to anticipate a line of questioning and to do so will detract from your job as a witness, which is to listen and respond effectively to the single question before you.

When You Should Not Give an Answer

There are a few conditions under which you should refuse to answer a question. These include:

> 1. When the question would invade attorney-client privilege. If this happens, your attorney will object and instruct you not to answer.

> 2. When you do not clearly and completely understand the question.

3. When answering the question requires you to guess, speculate, assume, or provide information that is outside your area of knowledge or expertise.

If you do not completely understand the question, ask for clarification. If you do not seek clarification, you cannot later declare that you are changing your answer because you did not understand it the first time it was asked. Recall that opposing counsel may have made the disclaimer that if you answer a question, it will be assumed you understood it. You can't cry foul later.

CHAPTER 11

SOME ADDITIONAL RULES FOR ANSWERING QUESTIONS

Many attorneys give their witnesses a list—some are short, some are long—about the "do's and don'ts" of testifying at a deposition or at trial. Even though you may acknowledge the importance of these rules, it's difficult to remember them all. The following list is fairly common and inclusive, but hopefully not too overwhelming.

Be Completely Honest

Without exception, be completely honest and forthcoming with your attorney, regardless of how sensitive, embarrassing, or upsetting the issues in the case. Unless you are completely candid with your attorney, he or she cannot effectively represent you. As any candidate for political office knows, there is little information that can be hidden in this era of social networking, YouTube, and instant text messaging. Be assured, however, that whatever is discussed with your attorney about your case is protected by law under the attorney-client privilege regarding confidentiality.

It goes without saying that in a deposition or at trial, always tell the truth, and do not fabricate, exaggerate, or misrepresent. If you are caught in even a small white lie, your entire testimony can be called into question and jurors can be instructed to disregard all of it. A truthful answer is always the best, even if you think it will weaken your case. If it is the truth, an admission is more credible than hedging or dodging the question.

Breathe

Pause and take in a breath of air between the question and your answer. This will force you to keep a slow and even pace. It will also give your attorney time to make an objection if one is warranted. Fast talkers are assumed to be trying to pull something over on people, so slow down and take your time. This is not the game show *Jeopardy* and there are no extra points for answering in a ratta-tat-tat fashion.

One Question at a Time

Answer only the question that is asked, and avoid trying to anticipate what the attorney will ask next. Don't explain "why" if you are asked a yes-or-no question. If you feel that bypasses an important explanation, you can add, for example: "Yes, I left the building at 8:00 AM, for several reasons." Chances are, you will be asked to give those reasons. If not, jurors will expect an explanation when your own attorney is questioning you. In a deposition, going off on tangents and explaining background or historical contexts is both inappropriate and annoying. It is doubly so at trial.

Use Ordinary Language

Avoid slang and jargon. It is not hip to be hip in court. The courtroom is a somber and conservative place, and using slang or contemporary jargon is viewed as a sign of disrespect. Unless you are giving a direct quote that includes slang or jargon, or you are making a specific point regarding word usage, stick to ordinary English. If you use professional acronyms (such as ROI, CDC, NASA, etc.) be certain to explain what the letters stand for. Don't assume that everyone will know the nuances of your professional or cultural language expressions.

Do Not Memorize

Don't attempt to memorize answers to questions you anticipate will be asked. Chances are you will forget the memorized answer and botch it.

Refer to Records

Any records or documents you need to look at in order to answer a question will be made available to you. Take time to review them if your memory needs to be refreshed, and refrain from talking while looking at written records or other documents. Most people mumble while reading and these utterances will go on the record along with your answers.

Speak Up

Speak loudly and clearly, as this reflects confidence. If you are trying to project an image of meekness and passivity, speaking quietly with your head lowered will not convey that message. You will only come across as intimidated, wimpy, and ineffective. Speak up so people can hear what you have to say.

Do Not Argue

While you should be persistent in ensuring your answers are precise, it is unwise to argue with an attorney, or to attempt to outwit him or her. They are likely much better at argument than you, and arguing only serves to make you look bad. You could get upset, distracted, and confused, and this will not help you. Take the high road. Answer questions truthfully without arguing. If you disagree with a statement made by opposing counsel, just say so: "I disagree with what you just said." Or say, "No, that is not how it happened." Simple disagreement is more effective than arguing. Arguing is often seen by jurors as defensive and perhaps a reflection of underlying feelings of guilt.

Stay in Your Box

In order to appear intelligent and competent, we all desire to give an answer to every question. But in reality, we simply don't have all the answers. "Staying in your box" simply means that you confine your answers to matters about which you have personal experience, training, expertise, or knowledge. What lies outside your box includes hypothetical situations, estimates and guesses, events you did not personally observe, documents authored by others, events in which you had no role, the personal thoughts of other people, opinions held by others, and knowledge you do not possess. Never venture outside your box to answer a question. Answering questions about things you don't know much about or have only passing familiarity with could conflict with the testimony of others who actually do have knowledge and experience in that area. Simply say, "I don't know" or "That is outside my area of expertise or experience" rather than guess or speculate. Unless you are giving testimony as an expert witness, your opinions are usually not relevant anyway. Only facts are.

Use Definitive Words

Avoid qualifiers such as "I think," "I guess," or "maybe." Prefacing your answers with these qualifiers detracts from the effectiveness of your answer. On the other hand, avoid beginning sentences with the words "Frankly…" or "Honestly…" Doing so suggests that at other times, you are not being frank or honest. These are difficult habits to break, and making yourself aware of these prefixes may help to curb them when giving testimony.

Vary Your Speech

Long, rambling answers are much less effective than short, succinct responses. Some people can speak for surprisingly long periods of time without seeming to take a breath. Jurors learn to tune out answers that seem to go on indefinitely with little point. Short, punchy sentences of ten-to-twelve words are much more effective. If your answer is expected to be long, break it up into several short sentences. Media professionals refer to these as "sound bites." Other ways of gaining and holding the attention of jurors include the following:

- Use your hands when speaking, as this adds energy to your words.
- Vary the pitch and tempo of your voice, as a slow monotone will put everyone to sleep.

- Use animated gestures to describe actions.

- Use words that create visual images, such as, "a knot on my head the size of a walnut," "the pressure was like an elephant sitting on my chest," "the fog was so heavy it seemed like a curtain had been dropped in front of the car," or "pain that feels like a hot knife is being jabbed into my back."

- Put up your fingers and tick off a list of points you wish to make or items you intend to discuss, such as "three things I do when I first get to work," or "four options I gave the patient for treating her knee problem."

Adding energy and a little animation to long answers will help keep jurors awake and attentive, especially after lunch or toward the end of a long day of testimony.

Watch Your Body Language

When giving testimony at a deposition or trial, maintain good posture and eye contact regardless of how long you have been questioned. Slouching in your chair, leaning your head in your hands, staring at the ceiling, swiveling, or rocking all convey the message that you are not taking the proceedings seriously, or that you are a "slouch" of a person. Even if you are tired or a little uncomfortable, sit up straight and look people in the eye. Posture and eye contact are some of the cues people use to judge your truthfulness and credibility. However, do not look to your attorney for answers or signals. This behavior tells attorneys, judges, and jurors that you are being programmed or coached by your attorney because you are fabricating answers. After giving a particularly good answer, don't look to your attorney for approval. Remember that *how* a witness testifies impresses jurors as much as the testimony itself.

Control Nervous Mannerisms

Use gestures when appropriate, but control distracting mannerisms such as hair twisting, blinking, frowning, eye rolling, head scratching, nail biting, foot tapping, and frequent removal and replacement of eyeglasses.

Such mannerisms are seen as signs of nervousness, indicating you are not telling the truth. If you cannot overcome a mannerism, make certain to explain that you are nervous because you have never testified before.

CHAPTER 12

GETTING THROUGH A TOUGH CROSS-EXAMINATION

Whether in a deposition or at trial, being cross-examined (that is, questioned by the attorney for the opposite side) is nerve-wracking. This is the kind of questioning most witnesses fear because it is the opposing side who is questioning you, and s/he can be expected to be thorough, detailed, and sometimes aggressive. Here are some tips on how to survive a challenging cross-examination.

Tip #1: Don't Change Your Demeanor

Jurors don't know what to think about witnesses who appear cooperative, patient, and likeable when being questioned by their own attorney, but who turn into angry, insolent, and rude people when being cross-examined. Keep the same calm and confident demeanor regardless of who is asking the question. Focus on the content of the question, not who is asking it or the tone they are using when phrasing it. Remember that at trial, the audience is the jurors, not the attorneys.

Tip #2: Answer in Full Sentences

Beginning at the very start of cross-examination, frame your answers as full sentences. Rather than answering with a quick yes or no, give an accurate, cooperative response in a full sentence. Jurors will have no basis for forming a positive impression if you reply to questions with one-word answers. Witnesses are under no obligation to restrict their answers to a single word. So even if told by opposing counsel that you should "Just answer yes or no," you can still make a full sentence: "Yes, that is correct." By using complete sentences, you establish your right to give full and complete answers. Full sentences also make people appear more relaxed and less like prisoners being interrogated by the enemy. However, rambling and going off on tangents should also be avoided.

If the opposing attorney insists on a yes or no response, but you know that to give a single word answer would be misleading, you can always say, "There is no simple yes or no answer. May I explain?" If you are instructed by the judge to give a yes or no response, you must do so. Your chance to explain may have to wait until your own attorney has an opportunity to seek clarification during his or her questioning of you.

Tip #3: Watch Out for the "Yes" Cycle

Be alert to a sequence of quick short questions in a row, to which the answer is a simple yes or no. You could get into a repetitive pattern that lulls you into answering the final question in the quick series incorrectly. Consider the following example:

> Q: *You knew, didn't you, that stacking the rolls of linoleum in the corner of the room could be a hazard, didn't you?*
>
> A: *Yes.*
>
> Q: *And you knew children would be playing in that area after you left the worksite, didn't you?*
>
> A: *Yes.*
>
> Q: *And you knew that if children played on the linoleum roles, this would be a serious risk to their safety, right?*
>
> A: *Yes.*

Q: *And you knew the linoleum rolls should be well secured to make sure children didn't hurt themselves, right?*

A: *Yes.*

Q: *So your failure to secure the linoleum rolls actually resulted in the death of Jimmy Doe, didn't it?*

A: *Yes.*

Lulled into a pattern of "yes" responses, the witness stopped listening to the specific questions and assumed they would all require an affirmative answer. In this example, the defendant mistakenly admitted liability because he had failed to control the pace and take time to listen to each question before responding.

Tip #4: Avoid "Yes, but…"

Any time a witness begins an answer with "Yes, but…" what comes after the "but" is largely ignored or heard as an excuse. The "Yes, but…" preface suggests you agree basically with the attorney, and everything that follows is quibbling. When faced with a question that requires a qualified answer, give the explanation first, before the affirmation. Here is an example:

Q: *You told Mr. Smith that he would have to catch up on his rent within four days or he would be evicted, didn't you?*

A: *I had given Mr. Smith several verbal and written warnings before that, so yes, I did tell him the last extension would expire in four days.*

It is a good idea to avoid the use of "but" in any answer. For example, here is an idea of how to substitute the word "and" (a more effective word) instead of "but" in giving an answer:

Q: *You didn't stop at the red light at the intersection of Fifth and Main on July 5 when you crashed into my client's car and caused serious injury, did you?*

Option #1: *I tried to stop, but I couldn't.* [All jurors hear is "tried" and "but."]

Option #2: *I stepped on the brake and I realized immediately that there was ice on the roadway and my brakes would fail.* [Jurors hear "ice" and "brakes failed."]

Option #1 used "but" and option #2 used "and," making it a more effective response. Remember that "but" has no place in an effective witness's vocabulary. For practice, try avoiding the use of "but" in all your conversations for the next few days and use only "and." You will be amazed at how much more effective your communications will be. Here is an example using a common relationship complaint:

Option #1: *I tried to explain, but you never let me get a word in edgewise.*

Option #2: *I tried to explain, and I got frustrated when you cut me off before I could finish.*

Tip # 5: Give Context If Appropriate

While it is always best to give succinct answers during cross-examination, there are times when a simple answer would be misleading or inaccurate. Consider the three optional answers and decide which one is most effective:

Q: *You didn't stop at the red light on the corner of 5th and Lovejoy before hitting Mr. Smith's car broadside, did you?*

Option #1: *No, I didn't.*

Option #2: *I didn't see the ice just before the intersection, so when I hit the ice patch I wasn't able to stop.*

Remember that even if you have not thought about the appropriate context warranted by the question, you can always ask for the opportunity to explain:

Option #3: *No, I didn't, and I would like to explain why.*

Even if your request to explain is denied by the attorney, you have alerted jurors that there is more to the story and they will wait to hear it when your attorney questions you.

Sometimes it may be necessary to not only deny the content of a question, but to suggest that something else may in fact be closer to the truth. Here is an example:

> Q: *Your crane tipped over and caused considerable damage at the plant. A crane that tips over on an uneven surface is not a safe crane, is it?*
>
> A: *The crane is safe. It has to be operated in a safe manner, and it was not.*

Note that the answer is not an argument; it is simply stating a fact that made the hypothetical question a more complete scenario.

Tip #6: Save It for Direct Examination

Many witnesses worry that they will not be allowed to give full explanations to cross-examination questions, and that if forced to limit their answers, the result will be misleading. In fact, you will likely be given few opportunities to expand on your answers while you are being cross-examined by opposing counsel. Don't worry. Your own attorney will later give you that opportunity. Think about it—when is the best time to give a full explanation? When your own attorney is asking you questions! So why not wait? If you are concerned that a brief answer will be misleading, plant a seed by suggesting there is more to the story. For example:

> Q: *You didn't complete the form that was required to be filled out before you called Child Protective Services, did you?*
>
> A: *No, for several good reasons.*

This answer suggests there is a more complete explanation, without the risk of being cut off by opposing counsel, who may not want jurors to hear the explanation. Jurors will be anxious to hear the full answer later, when your attorney is questioning you.

Tip #7: Use Safe Harbors When Necessary

Nearly every witness, at some point in a deposition or trial, will be at a loss for words. A responsive answer simply will not come to mind, for any number of reasons. When this occurs, use a life jacket or a safe harbor to protect yourself from an answer that could pull you under or out into deeper waters. Here is what we mean by safe harbors:

Examples of Safe Harbors

"It depends on the situation."

"I've given the best, most complete answer I can give on that issue."

"That question doesn't make sense to me. Can you ask it differently?"

"I'm not certain and I don't want to guess or speculate."

"I've never been asked that question before. I'll need a moment to think about it."

"I don't know the answer."

"I don't recall that [incident] with clarity."

"I don't have the job experience to answer that question."

The idea is that not all questions may be capable of being answered, or of being answered as asked. Use safe harbors judiciously and never use one as a means of dodging a difficult question.

Tip #8: Let Go of the Rope

Nearly all witnesses are uncomfortable when cross-examined about weaknesses in their case or about questionable actions. When an attorney pushes on you, the defensive instinct is to push back in order to defend yourself. But defensiveness can be misread by jurors and judges as an awareness of weaknesses in the case, guilt, or a lack of confidence in your answers. Even worse, it can signal others that you think the weakness is more important than it actually is.

Psychologist Stan Brodsky suggests that when you find yourself wanting to be defensive, use the tug-of-war strategy of "letting go of the rope." Here are some examples:

> Q: *Don't you wonder if you did everything possible to accommodate Ms. Smith when her medical condition began to affect her work?*
>
> A: *Of course I wonder. Even after we adjusted her workload and brought in a special chair, I still wonder if there is more we could have done.*
>
> Q: *Didn't you think about the safety of the public when you started squirting pepper spray into the group of demonstrators?*
>
> A: *Absolutely. It was our job to ensure the safety of everyone who could get hurt—not just the demonstrators but also any other people in close proximity.*
>
> Q: *The fact is, you didn't visit your father in the nursing home for several months before his death, did you?*
>
> A: *I did not, and I regret that I wasn't told how sick he was."*

Tip #9: Counteract Feelings of Shame and Guilt

Feelings of guilt and shame are aroused when an attorney suggests through his or her questioning that you failed to do something you should have. Feelings of remorse may be raised when the question from an attorney suggests you should feel badly about your actions or your inactions.

These kinds of questions are intended to prey on your own natural feelings of self-doubt, self-blame, and self-punishment. For example:

Q: *Your own research showed the use of Drug X could cause serious side effects, yet you kept this from the public, knowing this was wrong, didn't you?*

Q: *Your failure to diagnose Ms. Doe's cancer has left her family without a mother and wife, hasn't it?*

When asked such questions, most witnesses respond in one of two ways. They may become immediately defensive, talking rapidly and loudly, and denying the accusations. Or they admit their guilt by lowering their head and responding with weak apologies. Neither response will serve you well. The best response is to remind yourself that this is a lawyer tactic and you will not fall for it. Instead, respond with an accurate, confident answer. For example:

A: *Our research was not completed by December of 2008. At that time, we did not have sufficient data collected to alert the public about any serious side effects.*

A: *Even if diagnosed three months earlier, Ms. Doe's cancer was unfortunately already too far advanced to treat successfully.*

Tip #10: If You Feel Manipulated

There may be instances in the course of your examination when you feel opposing counsel is trying to manipulate your testimony, twist your words, or mischaracterize what you have said. When this happens, arguing is rarely effective. Most attorneys enjoy a good argument because they most often win them. The best response is a simple and direct one, such as:

"That mischaracterizes my testimony."

"That is not exactly what I said."

"I disagree completely."

"Just the opposite is what I intended to convey."

"Absolutely not."

"You have twisted my words and that strikes me as unfair."

Your demeanor when using one of these phrases will also be important. Speaking in an angry or offended tone of voice will detract from the impact; making a clear, calm statement magnifies its effect.

Tip #11: Don't Multitask

You may indeed be one of those talented people who can multitask: juggle while composing music, drive while applying makeup, write a report while on a conference call. But most people cannot. In your deposition, do not attempt to multitask by reading a report or a piece of correspondence while a question is being asked. If your head is buried in a document and you are searching for that important piece of information needed to answer a question, stop talking until you have found it. Then put the document aside and answer the question. No matter how intelligent or talented you may be, it is challenging to listen carefully, read for content, and formulate an answer simultaneously. There is no reason to try to do so. One thing at a time!

If you are given a document (a memo, medical chart note, contract, etc.) that you have not seen before, or haven't seen for some time, take the time to read it carefully before answering any questions about it. If you feel rushed to answer a question concerning a document, one possible way to respond might be to state politely, "To answer your question accurately, I will need a minute or two to read this. May I?" Then take all the time you need. If several minutes have elapsed, you may want to ask that the original question be repeated.

CHAPTER 13

TESTIFYING AS AN EXPERT

If you have been hired or contracted by an attorney to provide expert testimony in a case, you are already likely very familiar with what is expected of you. There are also a number of excellent books on the market written specifically for testifying experts. This chapter is included for experts who may simply need a brush-up on providing testimony at a deposition or trial.

Keep in mind that rules about the use of experts, the manner in which they are prepared to offer testimony, and the discoverability of their files and materials vary from jurisdiction to jurisdiction, and even between state and federal courts in the same jurisdiction. Rely upon the attorney who has retained you with regard to the specifics of your preparation. The information in this chapter is intended to be general and not case-specific.

What Jurors Say about Expert Witnesses

When jurors are asked in post-trial interviews whom they thought was the best expert (that is, the expert witness they listened to carefully, understood well, recalled the testimony of, and were most influenced by), they nearly always say, "The one who taught us best." When asked to explain what that meant to them, they often say the best expert was the one who:

- Used common language and did not talk over our heads by trying to impress us with his or her technical proficiency.

- Did not talk down to us as if we were second-graders.

- Gave his or her attention to us, not to the attorneys.

- Used demonstration materials to help us understand.

- Used analogies and examples that made sense to us.

- Admitted limitations and did not argue every point; was able to make concessions when necessary and appropriate; did not always have to win the point.

- Was not defensive about fees or past experience as an expert.

- Did not suffer under the weight of his or her own ego; appeared very confident without seeming arrogant.

- Spoke slowly so we could take notes, but was not annoyingly repetitive.

As an expert witness, the most important thing to remember when giving testimony in a legal proceeding is that in order to be influential, you must be heard, understood, believed, and recalled. Otherwise you are less effective than you would hope to be.

Some Brush-up Points

You will be questioned about your qualifications, education, experience, and publications. Bring a copy of the curriculum vitae with you, as it is often offered as an exhibit. That way, examination of your qualifications to give expert opinions may be shortened. Be prepared to provide a list of any attorneys and law firms you have worked with previously. You will be asked to specify how often you have worked for the defense and for the prosecution/plaintiffs. Be prepared to give a thumbnail sketch of all previous cases for which you were retained as an expert.

Be mindful of any former opinions you may have expressed that could conflict with your opinions in the present case. Be aware of statements you have made in any publication, or any publicly recorded opinions you have expressed previously. Under cross-examination, any contrary opinions you have expressed will be pointed out, in an attempt to expose inconsistencies. If this is true, be prepared to point out the differences between the current case and others.

You will be asked to recite a list and description of the materials you used in formulating your opinions in the case. Be prepared to explain and confidently defend your assumptions and conclusions that substantiate the opinions you express. Remember that any of the opinions you form should be based on "reasonable probability" or "reasonable certainty."

Avoid saying you "looked at" documents. Use powerful and descriptive words and phrases such as carefully read, examined closely, conducted a detailed review, or thoroughly analyzed. Use words that reflect your conscientiousness.

You may be asked to identify any colleagues with whom you have discussed your assumptions, conclusions, or opinions. Be aware that anyone you consulted in forming your opinions may also be questioned.

You will be asked to detail the specific issues you were asked to examine and consider in forming your opinions and conclusions. For example: the scene of an accident, the reliability of a piece of equipment, the policy and procedures manual of the clinic, the behavior of a person under stress, etc. You will be asked what documents, records, forms, or correspondence you were asked to review regarding those issues.

You will certainly be asked your fee for testifying in court or giving a deposition. You may be asked if this includes preparation time, travel expenses, travel time, telephone calls, etc. Be prepared to answer these questions in a straightforward manner. If you are asked "Are you being paid for your opinions here today?" the best response is "I am being paid for my time; my opinions are my own."

If you have put together a file or report pertaining to the case, any attorney involved in the case has a right to examine it. It may even be marked as an exhibit. You should retain your original documentation.

The opposing attorney's goal is to call into question your credentials (i.e., your qualifications to offer an expert opinion), to argue that the facts you were supplied are inadequate to support your conclusions, and/or to propose that the conclusions you have drawn are incorrect or ill-informed. Be prepared for vigorous cross-examination. Being a paid expert witness raises the bar in the eyes of jurors regarding how aggressively you can be questioned.

Simplify all technical jargon. The chief complaint of jurors regarding expert witnesses is that they "talked over our heads," resulting in a general tune-out by jurors who felt lost in the verbiage. Use layperson's terms, or state the term and then describe it in a way that the average fifteen-year-old could understand it. Explain things to jurors as you would to your spouse or children, or others who may know little of the technical aspects of your testimony. If they can't understand it, neither will jurors.

Use props, demonstrative aids, and visuals as much as possible. In the courtroom, a picture can truly be worth a thousand words. Visuals and demonstrations help simplify complex information and assist jurors to recall it. Whenever possible and appropriate, use models, diagrams, mock-ups, replicas, photos, video simulations, charts, instruments, and tools. Get out of the "I'm an important person" mode and into the "I'm a good teacher" mode. Jurors are less impressed with credentials than they are with the ability to help them understand complex facts.

If you are using a prop or other visuals, be certain to practice with them. Few things are more annoying to jurors than time wasted while a witness fusses with a non-working DVD or a model that falls apart in demonstration. Once, while attempting to show how a particular injection was done into a joint, the medical expert began shaking so obviously in front of the jurors that the intended point of the demonstration was lost. He had simply not prepared well by practicing the demonstration to the point of confidence. Don't allow that to happen to you.

Additional Resources

The best-known and most prolific author on preparing expert witnesses is Stanley L. Brodsky, and his self-help books can be located easily on any Internet bookseller site, such as Amazon.com.

APPENDIX

QUICK REVIEW
AND REFERENCE

The day or evening before you are scheduled to give a deposition or to provide testimony in a courtroom, it is a good idea to briefly review what you have learned in this book. It will refresh your memory and boost your confidence that you are well prepared and will do well at the deposition or on the stand. To make it easier for you, we have briefly summarized some major points. You have the authors' permission to copy this appendix and stick it on your mirror as you get ready the morning of your deposition or the day you will testify at trial.

Basic Rules for Deposition

1. Always tell the truth. Always.

2. Listen carefully to every word in the question.

3. Pause and take in a breath of air before answering.

4. Avoid absolute terms (such as always, never) that could box in your testimony.

5. Don't volunteer or educate outside the specific question being asked.

6. Aim to be precise, concise, and consistent.

7. Listen for traps, inflammatory words, and embedded assumptions.

8. Control the pace and take your time. Don't rush your answers.

9. Control your emotions. Emotions get in the way of clear thinking.

10. Sit up in the chair and make good eye contact.

11. Ask for clarification when needed. Never guess or assume or suppose.

12. Don't expect to know or remember everything. You are not perfect.

Basic Rules for Trial Testimony

1. Always tell the truth. Always.

2. You are in the jurors' sights at all times. Be on your best behavior.

3. Be a juror educator, not a witness.

4. Talk to the jurors and make eye contact. They are the decision-makers.

5. Avoid jargon, professional or otherwise, or else explain it.

6. Keep your demeanor the same, regardless of who is questioning you.

7. Listen carefully and pause before answering.

8. Speak with some animation, not a monotone. Create mental pictures.

9. Tell your story. Now is the time to talk and explain and educate.

10. Show your respect for the court. Act and dress appropriately and groom properly.

ABOUT THE AUTHORS

Angela M. Dodge, Ph.D., is the founding partner of Dodge Consulting and Publications LLP, a litigation consulting practice based in the Seattle-Tacoma area. An experienced trial consultant and social psychologist, she assists hundreds of attorneys across the country with witness preparation, juror-sensitive trial strategy, jury selection, pre-trial research (focus groups and mock trials), and post-trial juror interviews. She has assisted in a wide range of civil cases, from personal injury and professional malpractice, to employment issues and patent infringement. Dr. Dodge has prepared several thousand witnesses, from corporate executives to hospital aides. Her expertise in the areas of courtroom communications and jury persuasion has enabled her to consult on high-profile cases involving tobacco, breast implants, sexual abuse of children, automotive defects, environmental cleanup, police shootings, and pharmaceuticals. She has special expertise in the area of medical malpractice defense. She is the author of *When Good Doctors Get Sued: A Practical Guide for Physicians Involved in Malpractice Lawsuits* (ISBN 978-0-977751105), *Winning at Jury Selection* (ISBN 978-0-977751143), and *Preparing Witnesses to Give Effective Testimony: The Attorney's Essential Guide* (ISBN 978-0-977751167). She has a solid reputation as a consultant and seminar speaker.

John H. Ryan, Ph.D., is a senior partner at Dodge Consulting and Publications LLP. Trained as a clinical psychologist, he has applied his thirty-plus years of experience in group and individual counseling to the practice of preparing witnesses for deposition and trial, conducting pre-trial research, and assisting with jury selection in a variety of cases. He has special expertise in litigation stress management, and has provided consultation on trial and jury selection strategy to both plaintiff and defense counsel. Dr. Ryan has a stellar reputation for working successfully with highly anxious or otherwise challenging witnesses, and with those who are particularly intimidated by the litigation process. He has assisted in the preparation of hundreds of professionals, with an emphasis on healthcare providers and corporate executives. In addition to this book, he is co-author of *Preparing Witnesses to Give Effective Testimony: The Attorney's Essential Guide* (ISBN 978-0-977751167). Prior to his career as a therapist and litigation consultant, he served honorably as a USAF pilot in Vietnam, and then worked with at-risk youth as a juvenile probation officer.